THE
YOUNG IRELAND
REBELLION
AND LIMERICK

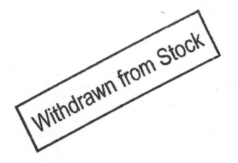

THE YOUNG IRELAND REBELLION AND LIMERICK

LAURENCE FENTON

MERCIER PRESS
IRISH PUBLISHER – IRISH STORY

MERCIER PRESS

Cork

www.mercierpress.ie

Trade enquiries to CMD BookSource,
55a Spruce Avenue, Stillorgan Industrial Park,
Blackrock, County Dublin

© Laurence Fenton, 2010

ISBN: 978 1 85635 660 2

10 9 8 7 6 5 4 3 2 1

A CIP record for this title is available from the British Library

Printed and bound in the EU.

CONTENTS

Acknowledgements

This book has been a number of years in gestation. For their support and encouragement during this period, my deepest thanks go to my close friends and family, especially my mother Eileen.

For permission to refer to manuscripts and for assistance during the course of this work, my thanks are due to a number of organisations and individuals: the Royal Irish Academy; the board of the National Library of Ireland; the board and director of the National Archives of Ireland; the board of Trinity College, Dublin; the Cork City and County Archives; the Special Collections Library at University College, Cork; Chris Woolgar of the University of Southampton; Jacqui Hayes of Limerick City Archives; Brian Hodkinson of Limerick City Museum; and Mike Maguire of Limerick City Library.

I am also grateful to Mervyn O'Driscoll for his help in any number of historical endeavours over the years, to all at Mercier Press and to Eoin Purcell.

INTRODUCTION

The early months of 1848 saw a spectacle of revolution across Europe. Gustave Flaubert, who walked the streets of revolutionary Paris, wove the sights and sounds of the barricades into his great novel *Sentimental Education*. Giuseppe Verdi's opera *La Battaglia di Legnano*, though based on a twelfth-century conflict, was inspired by the patriotic fervour of the 'year of revolutions'; its premiere in Rome in January 1849 brought the audience to a 'frenzy of enthusiasm', with repeated cries of 'Viva Italia'. Frédéric Chopin's last public appearance, in October 1848, was at a charity concert in London for Polish refugees, whilst Franz Liszt's magnificent elegy *Funérailles* was composed in the aftermath of the failed Hungarian uprising and paid tribute to the dead leaders of that rebellion. The Italian revolutionary, Giuseppe Garibaldi, meanwhile, has been lionised in the poetry of writers as far removed from the rebellions as Herman Melville.[1]

The Young Ireland rebellion of 1848 was a secondary but still significant member of this family of revolutions. It has, however, been glanced over in many surveys of the period, and its main protagonists have hardly been celebrated in popular culture. An exception to this is Liam O'Flaherty's 1937 novel *Famine*, which contains a wonderful account of the character Thomsy Hynes' brief encounter with a Young Irelander in a barn in the west of Ireland. The fair-haired Young Irelander, to Thomsy's fragile mind, was a 'powerful man' with a voice 'as clear as a bell' and full of inspirational talk of an army and a republic, as well as landlords being 'shot down like rabbits'.[2]

Much of the work on the rebellion this 'bold hero' was engaged in has been too narrowly focused on the activities of the Young Ireland leadership in Dublin, whilst ignoring the mobilisation that took place among ordinary Irish people beyond the capital.[3] This book will explore the manner in which the men and women of Limerick reacted to the tumultuous year of revolutions: how some, inspired by the news coming from Paris, took to the streets to sing songs of rebellion while others cowered at the prospect of upheaval, caring only about filling their famine-starved bellies. It will add a rich, local flavour to the literature on 1848.

1

'SECESSION'

The walls of Conciliation Hall, the 'quietly elegant' headquarters of the Repeal Association in Dublin, were decorated with pictures of Irish wolfhounds, round towers and other symbols of Gaelic iconography. A harp and two shamrocks stood out in low relief from the centre of the high ceiling, and twelve bronze candelabra lit the proceedings. At the head of the hall, the chairman of the meeting peered down on events from a raised platform; the hall was crowded to excess, with various classes of repealers seated according to the value of their subscriptions. The journalists, packed together near the stage, transcribed quickly all that was said. It was Tuesday 28 July 1846, the second day of an increasingly rancorous debate, and tempers that had been held in check during the first afternoon had started to fray, the two factions of the association, 'Young Ireland' and 'Old Ireland', competing to shout each other down.[1]

Struggling to be heard above the din of cheers and hisses was Thomas Francis Meagher. One of the leading Young Irelanders, Meagher, from Waterford, was just twenty-two years old, but had already earned a reputation of being a fine speaker. In a slightly English accent, picked up at university, he reaffirmed his support for the 'peaceful policy' of the association. At the same time, however, Meagher insisted that he could not pledge himself – as was being demanded – 'to the unqualified repudiation of physical force in all countries, at all times, and in every circumstance'. There were, he averred, many honourable examples of armed resistance to power, when the fight for national rights called out 'for a drop of blood – and many thousand drops of blood'.[2]

Two weeks earlier, Daniel O'Connell, the fêted 'Liberator' of Ireland, had tabled a provocative set of motions – the 'peace resolutions' – repudiating physical force 'in *any event* and in any contingency'.[3] O'Connell, a lawyer and landowner from County Kerry, was one of the great political figures of the era: a tall, broad-chested folk hero who had won the campaign for Catholic emancipation in Ireland. His final crusade – repeal of the Act of Union of 1801 – had witnessed a series of huge political gatherings across the country. At these 'monster meetings', an ageing but still remarkably robust O'Connell demanded self-government for Ireland. O'Connell was utterly opposed to the use of violence in politics, his repeal movement a mirror of the earlier emancipation campaign in its focus on 'people power' and 'moral force'. He was disturbed, therefore, when a section of younger repealers, grouped mainly around the influential *Nation* newspaper, became increasingly bellicose in their language. This trend reached its apogee, in O'Connell's eyes, in an article suggesting railway defiles (steep-sided, narrow passages) were ideal places for ambushing British forces. Another article, published in the early months of 1846, declared of an insurrection in Poland: 'Better a little blood-letting to show that there is blood, than a patient dragging of chains.'[4] These so-called Young Irelanders – middle-class and literary-minded nationalists – had established themselves as a powerful cohort in the repeal movement, challenging the previously indomitable O'Connell on repeal tactics and policy.

O'Connell was genuinely concerned that the militant tone of the *Nation* might prompt the British authorities to prosecute the Repeal Association for sedition. The three months he had spent in prison during the summer of 1844 on a charge of conspiracy had naturally increased his wariness in this regard. O'Connell objected to the articles very loudly, but also saw in the quarrel an opportunity for resolving his differences with the increasingly dissentient Young Irelanders: the peace resolutions, he freely admitted, were an attempt 'to draw a marked line between Young Ireland and Old Ireland'.[5] He would rein them in or force them out.

The Young Irelanders were at first unsure as to how they should respond to O'Connell's challenge – a confusion soon resolved in the heat of debate. They were accused of dragging repealers down the path of Danton, 'the bloody French revolutionist, who presided at the massacre not only of the aristocracy, but of thousands of the humble people'. John Mitchel – author of the articles that had so angered O'Connell

– tried to inject a sense of reality into the meeting. There was no question, he insisted, of the Young Irelanders desiring bloodshed or immediate insurrection; they were simply opposed to the dogmatic nature of O'Connell's stance. The Old Irelanders – their passions inflamed – shouted him down with cries of 'Old Ireland forever'.[6]

It was at this point that young Meagher rose to speak. He labelled the sword a 'sacred weapon', recalling a tale from the Bible where God 'nerved the arm of the Jewish girl' in Bethulia 'to smite the drunken tyrant in his tent'. Warming to his theme, he extolled the exploits of the American and Belgian revolutionaries of 1776 and 1830. Amid tumult and cheers, Meagher concluded, famously:

> Abhor the sword and stigmatise the sword? No, my lord, for at its blow a giant nation sprung up from the waters of the far Atlantic, and by its redeeming magic the fettered colony became a daring free Republic. Abhor the sword and stigmatise the sword? No, my lord, for it scourged the Dutch marauders out of the fine old towns of Belgium, back into their own phlegmatic swamps; and knocked their flag, and laws, and sceptre, and bayonets, into the sluggish waters of the Scheldt.

An infuriated John O'Connell – the third son and political heir of the Liberator – stopped Meagher from proceeding (Daniel O'Connell was absent from the meeting, being in London). For the younger O'Connell, Meagher's 'dangerous expressions' were an affront to his father. He called for an immediate vote 'to say yea or nay to the resolutions', and indicated that either the 'association must cease to exist, or Mr Meagher cease to be a member of it'.[7]

William Smith O'Brien – a Protestant landlord and Member of Parliament for County Limerick – was the next to rise. A late convert to repeal but, nonetheless, a prominent figure in the association, he remained unattached so far to either faction. In London, in late April 1846, he had refused to sit on a parliamentary committee dealing with railway construction in Scotland, citing a determination to work only on Irish affairs. Smith O'Brien was charged with contempt and imprisoned in a special room on the ground floor of the House of Commons for four weeks. The return to Limerick in early June of this tall, athletic figure with dark-brown hair was an occasion for immense celebration, Smith O'Brien being carried through the city on a triumphal chair that had been modelled on the chariots of Roman generals.[8] Smith O'Brien's incarceration in the House of Commons had been far from uncomfortable: his rooms were clean and commodious, and he had been allowed to take outside walks, attend church services and receive all the visitors he desired. The consequences of his detention, however, would prove more serious. The O'Connells – who had disagreed with his stance – were lukewarm in their support. Smith O'Brien consequently railed against the 'O'Connell creatures' in letters to his wife Lucy. In her reply, she described how she 'was boiling over with indignation at the way in which "that clique" had treated you'. She condemned the 'cunning & jealous mind of the Master', and praised those involved with the *Nation*.[9] The Young Irelanders had supported Smith O'Brien wholeheartedly during his imprisonment, and the debt he felt he owed them combined that fateful afternoon in Conciliation Hall with his own opposition to the peace resolutions and sundry other aspects of O'Connell's leadership. He rejected John O'Connell's ultimatum as a mean-spirited attempt to quell free discussion. Meagher's 'course of argument', he contended, 'was perfectly fair and legitimate'. John O'Connell returned to the floor and again condemned Meagher's 'most dangerous' language. Shouts of 'O'Connell, O'Connell' filled the air as Smith O'Brien – a member of one of the most illustrious clans in all of Ireland and a descendent of the fabled Munster chieftain Brian Boru – rose and left the building.[10]

Smith O'Brien was followed out of Conciliation Hall by a trail of Young Irelanders, among them Meagher, the well-dressed, charismatic young orator who revelled in the sobriquet 'Meagher of the Sword'; Mitchel, the thirty-year-old solicitor from County Down, the asthmatic son of a Presbyterian minister and firebrand writer for the *Nation*; Thomas Devin Reilly, a twenty-two-year-old Catholic from Monaghan town, County Monaghan, who had moved to Dublin with his family, then entered Trinity, but soon 'flung off his student's gown and threw himself into the wreck of the national cause'; Fr John Kenyon, a thirty-four-year-old parish priest in Templederry, County Tipperary, described later by the Fenian John O'Leary as 'simply the best talker, in whatever sense you use the word, I ever heard'; and P.J. Smyth, 'a young man with a small, pointed beard, cloak thrown back, silk hat in hand, the very personification of romantic adventure'.[11]

Other prominent Young Irelanders included Charles Gavan Duffy, the editor of the *Nation*. Duffy had co-founded this hugely popular newspaper in October 1842 with John Blake Dillon and Thomas Davis. The *Nation*'s mix of heroic ballad poetry and strident politics had reinvigorated a staid Irish newspaper scene. Davis, a Protestant, was the chief writer of the *Nation* before his untimely death in September 1845. Described by Mitchel as the 'very heart and soul' of Young Ireland, his presence would permeate all their lives long after his passing. Dillon was a thirty-two-year-old Catholic from County Roscommon, tall and 'dark as a Spaniard in complexion, with regular noble features and great melancholy eyes'. Duffy, a Catholic from Monaghan town, was thirty years old and more of an organiser than an orator, but an ardent nationalist nonetheless. Michael Doheny, an experienced agitator from County Tipperary, was another important figure, as was Richard O'Gorman junior, a twenty-five-year-old barrister from Dublin possessed of 'a fine presence and melodious accent'.[12]

A crowd waiting outside Conciliation Hall on Burgh Quay (near present-day O'Connell Bridge) cheered the Young Irelanders as they emerged from the building. Later that evening, however, Meagher was involved in a brawl with an Old Irelander named Captain Broderick, who had been among those most vocal in shouting him down. Smith O'Brien's jottings in his notebook that night were a study in pithy understatement: 'Adjourned meeting at Conciliation Hall. Secession.'[13]

2

'THE MURDERERS OF O'CONNELL'

Reports on Saturday 20 February 1847 that Daniel O'Connell was dead threw the residents of Limerick city into a state of confusion. The *Limerick and Clare Examiner* printed that evening's edition in thick, black mourning bands as a mark of respect. Large crowds – still unsure of the veracity of the story – gathered outside Cruise's Hotel to wait for the day coach from Dublin. The coach, however, was several hours late – a frequent occurrence, with horses foundering on the roads of Kildare or Tipperary and poles snapping in the bogs – and did not arrive until one o'clock in the morning, when it was preceded into town by 'the cheers of the people' announcing 'the safety of O'Connell'.[1] The story was false.

The rumour of O'Connell's death had originated in a letter sent home from London – where the Liberator was attending parliament – by a son of the Limerick businessman John Norris Russell. The story spread quickly, causing disquiet because it was so credible. O'Connell was seventy-one years old, and his health – declining since his spell in prison in 1844 – had deteriorated badly during the last months of 1846. His close friend William Joseph O'Neill Daunt was 'greatly struck' by the 'physical decay' of O'Connell after a visit in late 1846.[2] The powerful figure from the monster meetings of the early 1840s was no more.

Despite his failing health, O'Connell maintained his primacy in Irish politics during the winter of 1846–47. He engaged in some half-hearted negotiations with the Young Irelanders, but these broke down quickly. His chief focus during these physically trying months was on counteracting the effects of the Famine, then entering its second year. O'Connell, fully aware of his tenuous hold on life, was deeply troubled by the suffering of his people. Political objectives such as repeal were discarded, and his final appearance in the House of Commons on 8 February 1847 was a poignant sight, O'Connell trembling as he stood, his once-mighty voice barely carrying to a few rows before him. He did not declaim or exhort, assail or demand. Instead, the 'Great Dan' meekly begged of parliament that it 'interfere generously, munificently – he would say enormously – for the rescue of his country'.[3] It was a plea the Whig government of Lord John Russell – ardent subscribers to the dogma of *laissez-faire* economics – could not comprehend, much less respond to.

In the aftermath of this unsuccessful last stand in parliament, an ailing and increasingly devout O'Connell was advised by doctors to recuperate in a warmer climate, and he seized on this recommendation as an opportunity to make a pilgrimage to Rome. This was a daunting journey for a man of O'Connell's infirmity and age; he therefore travelled in slow, easy stages, sailing from Folkestone to Boulogne on 22 March, and not reaching Italy until early May. In Genoa, O'Connell stopped eating and became delirious, shouting out at his old adversary, Sir Robert Peel. The Liberator received the last rites from the leading clergy of the city, and died on the evening of Saturday 15 May.

The news of O'Connell's death – this time true – reached Limerick on the morning of Wednesday 26 May. A number of shops closed their doors, and the flags of vessels in the port flew at half-mast. An edge of controversy crept into proceedings when the dean of St Mary's cathedral refused a request from the mayor to toll the bells for O'Connell. The cathedral – one of the most important and historic buildings in the city – had been a Catholic place of worship before the Reformation. The nationalist *Limerick Reporter* advised the dean against goading the inhabitants of the city lest his actions remind them 'they are refused the use of the Bells of their own Cathedral of which they have been robbed by their *Sasanach* invaders'. The *Reporter* heaped praise on O'Connell, calling his death a 'national calamity', and insisting no 'pen or tongue' could do justice to his gifts. It lauded him as an 'Apostle of Peace' and 'one of the greatest men the world ever saw'. The *Reporter*, however, was a Young Ireland-supporting newspaper, and was quite infuriated with the reaction of the Old Irelanders, who seemed to be taking advantage of the

Liberator's death. It contrasted the 'genuine and sincere' grief of the Young Irelanders with the false sorrow of the 'parasites' at Conciliation Hall, who were busy branding the Young Irelanders the 'murderers of O'Connell'.[4]

THE 'HUNGRY FORTIES'

The Italy Daniel O'Connell had expired in was still reeling – like most of Europe – from the series of failed harvests that had plagued the middle years of the 1840s, and a potato blight that had spread across the Continent. The cost of basic foodstuffs such as cereals and bread increased dangerously, forcing some villagers in the south of Italy to eat the carcasses of donkeys found dead by the sides of roads.[5] The suffering caused by these agricultural failures was compounded by wider changes in society. Europe itself was in transition: a turbulent convulsion brought on by industrialisation, overpopulation and a great shift from country to city living. Food shortages and unemployment became the dominant motifs of a period that would be known as the 'Hungry Forties'.

The potato blight was continent-wide, but struck hardest in Ireland, where up to a third of the population was dependent on the crop for its survival. The blight appeared first in September 1845, turning half the potatoes in the country into a putrid, black mass, and precipitating a holocaust that in the course of six years saw at least a million people die of starvation and related diseases. The west-coast counties – including Limerick –

experienced the worst ravages of the Famine: extensive hunger, destitution and crime. Accounts from Croom spoke of 'emaciated corpses, partly green from eating docks, and partly blue from the cholera and dysentery'. A mill owner in Shanagolden, meanwhile, was assassinated because locals thought he was charging too much for corn.[6]

The more prosperous eastern half of County Limerick fared little better, with a pay clerk from the Board of Works robbed of £320 in Annacotty. There were also countless midnight raids on livestock; for example, in May 1847 'an armed party with their faces blackened' broke into the home of a farmer named Madigan, near Bruff. They attacked the farmer and his wife with the butts of their guns, and turned the place over in a search for money. The raiders stayed on in the house for more than two hours. They ate bread and veal, and 'regaled themselves' and joked even as blood poured from the heads of their victims, departing at last with bedclothes, jewellery and 'a few shillings'.[7]

Limerick city was spared the worst excesses of the Famine, thanks in part to its bacon factories, whose offal provided something of a bulwark against starvation. Food riots were not uncommon, however; a newspaper report in the summer of 1847 detailed how 'a large mob, consisting for the most part of women and boys' attacked several bakers' shops in the city, assaulting the workers with stones and tin cans, and making off with flour and bread. An influx of impoverished rural workers, meanwhile, led to overcrowding in the workhouses and poorer districts of the city – an area vividly described by the English novelist William Makepeace Thackeray in 1842 as 'a labyrinth of busy swarming poverty' with every house 'a half ruin' and 'swarming with people'.[8] This crush of people, combined with unsanitary conditions, made Limerick susceptible to contagious diseases, and in spring 1849 it suffered one of the deadliest outbreaks of cholera of the famine period in the country.

The distress of the 'Hungry Forties' – the social dislocation and economic depression, the urban squalor and rural poverty – proved fertile territory for revolutionists and agitators throughout Europe. Radical voices such as those of Giuseppe Mazzini – founder of the much-imitated 'Young Italy' movement – and Karl Marx, found new and receptive audiences in men like the character Deslauriers from Flaubert's *Sentimental Education*, who longed for a 'new 1789' and who was 'tired of constitutions, charters, subtleties, lies!' Defenders of the conservative old order seemed paralysed in the face of the great mood for change. Fr Joachim Ventura, officiating at the funeral mass for O'Connell in Rome prior to the return of his body to Ireland, seemed to give voice to their deepest fears when he spoke of a 'revolution which threatens to encompass the globe'.[9]

THE CASE OF IRELAND STATED

The Young Irelanders were far behind their contemporaries in Europe in terms of plotting and revolutionary ardour, and were instead focused on legal means of opposition to the Act of

Union, despite ostentatiously honouring the 'sword'. This preference was made clear at the inaugural meeting of the Irish Confederation, the new body set up by the Young Irelanders in January 1847. William Smith O'Brien, catapulted somewhat reluctantly into a leader-ship role, began proceedings with reference to a pamphlet, *The Case of Ireland Stated*, which supported Young Ireland. The author of this pamphlet, Robert Holmes, was a distinguished eighty-one-year-old lawyer and nationalist. He had defended United Irishmen in court in 1798 and was a brother-in-law of Robert Emmet, hanged in 1803; thus Holmes' *imprimatur* linked the Young Irelanders directly with these two revolts. The confederation, however, was as much an educational organisation as a political one – a point emphasised by Smith O'Brien when he spoke of the leaders delivering lectures all over the country. Public meetings, not underground conspiracies, would be their *modus operandi*.

The establishment of the confederation at a meeting in the Rotunda in Dublin had formalised – after several months of inertia – the split between Young and Old Ireland. Its first session was such a powerful antidote to the stasis of the previous six months that an exultant Richard O'Gorman exclaimed: 'Thank God! Sir, we are back at work. Thank God! We have flung behind us the quarrel that was embittering our feelings, and wasting away our strength.' O'Gorman then read out the names of those on the (rather inflated) thirty-six-member council of the confederation – the ruling body of the organisation – among them Smith O'Brien, John Mitchel and Thomas Meagher. William Griffin, a Limerick doctor and close friend of Smith O'Brien's, was offered a seat on the council but declined because he would be unable to attend enough meetings.[10]

The ultimate goal of the new organisation – repeal of the Act of Union and self-government for Ireland – was identical to that of the Repeal Association. Smith O'Brien's opening address, however, made clear some of the important differences between the two bodies. The confederation, he promised, would unite all classes and creeds behind repeal: landlords and labourers, Catholics and Protestants, north and south. It would be more genuinely welcoming of Protestants than the overtly Catholic Repeal Association, therefore 'practising' what the Old Irelanders merely 'preached' about non-sectarianism. It would also be more open to working-class members, holding meetings in the evening instead of the middle of the day, as was the case in Conciliation Hall. Furthermore, the confederation would be completely independent of all political parties in England – a sharp distinction from Daniel O'Connell, whose alliance with the Whigs in the summer of 1846 had so maddened the Young Irelanders at the time of their secession. Another important difference at this time of financial hardship was that while subscriptions were always welcome, admission to the confederation did not depend on the payment of a fee.

William Fuller Hartnett – the owner of a large clothes store in Newcastle West, County Limerick – was among the first subscribers to the Irish Confederation. The organisation, however, failed to make any serious impact on Irish politics during the early months of its existence. There was a degree of confusion among the leadership, a number of whom still harboured thoughts of rejoining a reformed Repeal Association. Charles Gavan Duffy was clearly aware of this problem when he wrote to a friend in December 1846; the Young Irelanders, he said, needed to move 'like Wordsworth's cloud' – 'all together or not all'.[11]

The Old Irelanders seemed unsure about their response to the confederation. Their mouthpiece, the *Pilot*, was utterly condescending towards the 'Little Ireland Gathering', but calmer heads – among them Sir Colman O'Loghlen – remained alert to the value of men of the calibre of Smith O'Brien and Meagher. The association was also struggling badly for funds in the midst of the Famine and with its unpopular alliance with the Whigs. O'Connell, in his last months, had been compelled to put up some of his own money to keep the association afloat.[12]

The confused focus of the Irish Confederation meant that the Young Irelanders were unable to defend themselves properly when, in the aftermath of O'Connell's death, the Repeal Association went on the offensive and let loose volleys of abuse towards the confederation, including the repeated claim that the confederates had broken the heart of O'Connell. They were clearly intent on exacting as much political capital as possible out of an outpouring of grief that, instead, could have been used as a prelude to political reconciliation and national regeneration.

AN 'OCCASION OF DEEP SORROW'

The mourners knelt down as one on the cold stone of Dublin harbour to watch Daniel O'Connell's huge, red-velvet-draped coffin being brought ashore. The black cloth from the temporary chapel on board the steamer was 'torn up in small fragments' and distributed among the thousands of onlookers seeking 'the smallest relic connected with the remains of the revered Liberator'. O'Connell lay in state for three days before burial in Glasnevin cemetery in Dublin on Thursday 5 August 1847, eleven weeks after his passing in Genoa.[13]

O'Connell's death had put the Young Irelanders in a politically awkward position. To avoid any hint of impropriety, the Irish Confederation postponed a number of meetings and asked members to 'wear some emblem of mourning upon their persons'.[14] By contrast, the Repeal Association – revitalised by renewed attention and an inflow of funds – saw the Liberator's death as an opportunity to kill off the challenge of the Young Irelanders, and delayed the repatriation of his body until just days before the general election of August 1847, when MPs would be chosen for Westminster.

Fr John Kenyon was one of the few Young Irelanders who refused to adopt a platitudinous stance. He criticised the glorifying tone of the *Nation*, and did not think O'Connell's death 'an occasion of deep sorrow'. O'Connell, to Kenyon's mind, was a scheming politician who had sold out the Irish people by forming an alliance with the Whigs. The confederation's acquiescence in the public honouring of his remains, he claimed, would be used 'to cut your own throats, & what is worse (for you deserve it) to cut the throat of your country'. Kenyon was vilified in the Conciliation Hall press for his comments. The priest – undaunted – renewed his attack a few months later, and labelled John O'Connell, the Liberator's son, 'a slave and a tyrant'.[15]

This incredible outburst of Kenyon's, just a day before O'Connell's burial, occurred during the course of a highly charged meeting in Limerick courthouse to choose candidates to stand in the forthcoming general election. The outcome was supposed to be a *fait accompli*, with the two Repeal Association candidates, John O'Brien and John O'Connell, expecting to be nominated to take the two seats for the city without any hint of opposition. Samuel Dickson, the only other candidate of note, had pulled out of the contest a few days earlier. Martin Honan nominated John O'Brien, a sitting MP. Thomas Wallnutt, the mayor, then put forward the name of the Liberator's son. Both Old Irelanders were quickly seconded.

It was at this point that Fr Kenyon stepped forward to speak, only to be interrupted by a man named Coleman – a 'pig jobber' – who described in a loud and menacing voice how he would 'knock out' the priest's eyes. The sheriff and some other priests eventually quietened the crowd – at least, until Kenyon called John O'Connell a 'despot' not worthy 'of the vote of any honest man'. Kenyon, who had been born in Limerick city, was opposed to John O'Connell because of his refusal to speak out against 'place-hunting', whereby a large number of Repeal Association MPs had accepted comfortable government sinecures once in parliament – a practice despised by Young Irelanders. Kenyon told those assembled that they had been used as pawns for too long 'by scheming politicians', and urged them to support a man 'unstained by Saxon gold'. He proposed Richard O'Gorman, despite an earlier decision by the Young Irelanders not to field candidates (they had decided to concentrate on obtaining pledges against place-hunting). O'Gorman, in Dublin, did not even want to be nominated.

The sheriff asked those backing the two Old Ireland nominees to raise their arms, and a 'whole forest' of hands filled the air. When he called on the supporters of O'Gorman, Kenyon 'held up his hand alone' in an attitude 'of calm and defiance against the derision and shouts of the populace'. He was, the *Reporter* suggested, 'a picture for Maclise', the famous Irish painter. The sheriff declared the meeting to be in favour of the two Conciliation Hall nominees. As the only candidates to have been seconded, there would in normal circumstances have been no need for a formal election. Kenyon, however, demanded an election. As his candidate had not been seconded, Kenyon was informed that he would have to pay the costs of the election. Undaunted, he set off to raise the funds, enduring shoving and jostling on his way out of the courthouse. The sheriff, meanwhile, arranged for polling booths to be set up in the courthouse and potato market.[16]

The voting for the general election in Limerick city took place over the two days following Kenyon's intervention. A large crowd gathered outside the courthouse on the evening of Friday 6 August to hear the results. The 'crush towards the door' broke through the ranks of the police and filled the hall to its limits. Adherents of both sides cheered and jeered as appropriate, the Old Irelanders making fun of the pomade used by Young Irelanders in their hair. The confederates, in return, called the Old Irelanders 'bog-trotters' only 'fit to frighten cows'. From an electorate of just over 2,000 – men who owned or rented property of at least £10 annual valuation – John O'Connell and John O'Brien garnered 583 and 537 votes apiece. O'Gorman achieved a miserable tally of thirty-seven. Kenyon's parting words to those gathered were as angry and bitter as before: 'You have acted like a set of savages. You are slaves and your children's children deserve to be slaves.'

The result in Limerick had been a foregone conclusion, the Young Irelanders entering the race far too late and making no canvass of electors. Nevertheless, a stand of sorts had been made, and Kenyon was described in the correspondence of Young Irelanders as having acted 'heroically'. The confederates in Limerick also established a fund to defray his expenses; William Smith O'Brien donated a very generous £10.[17]

'REPEAL AND NO COMPROMISE'

William Smith O'Brien, as the popular sitting MP for County Limerick, was an exception to the Young Ireland rule against fielding candidates in the general election. He was expected to compete for and win one of the two seats in his constituency. As ever with Smith O'Brien, events did not follow the simple path. He was completely disillusioned with parliament and tired of the long absences from his burgeoning family in Cahirmoyle in west Limerick. He gave a lot of thought to not running at all and even attacked his old acquaintance Caleb Powell, his ostensible running mate, as a 'repeal place-hunter' more dangerous to Ireland than any Whig or Tory. This criticism earned Smith O'Brien the full wrath of the Old Irelanders, who called him a 'rogue' and a 'murderer' during an emotive meeting in Limerick. Deeply hurt that no one at the meeting (chaired by the O'Connellite mayor, Thomas Wallnutt) challenged this last scandalous accusation, Smith O'Brien withdrew from the election. The situation was so intense, one alarmed correspondent even warned Smith O'Brien that 'a number of persons in Limerick are sworn to take your life'.[18]

Despairing of Irish politics and weary of the internecine strife, Smith O'Brien went off on a holiday to the Lake District in England. He then sailed across to the north of Ireland, and was in Donegal at the time of voting. The *Limerick Reporter* highlighted the easy, aristocratic life and the myriad honours bestowed on pliant peers that Smith O'Brien had given up by fighting for repeal. It must, the newspaper believed, have been 'peculiarly galling' to Smith O'Brien's sensitive mind to receive such a 'base return' from a people he had served 'so faithfully, and so long'. The article, however, also hinted that moves were afoot to have him nominated *in absentia*.[19]

John McClenahan, the editor of the *Reporter*, was one of Smith O'Brien's staunchest allies during the next, turbulent, few weeks. He was abused by Old Irelanders for his writings and even needed the protection of priests at one particularly heated meeting. McClenahan – who was among the older set of Young Ireland supporters – had worked on a number of liberal and nationalist papers in the north of Ireland, including the *Downshire Chronicle* and the *Newry Examiner*, before relocating to Limerick. In 1843 he coined the popular adage: 'That if a man had a coat and no pike, he should sell the coat and get a pike'. As editor of the *Reporter*, and whilst still advocating union of the repeal factions, McClenahan was clearly on the side of the Young Irelanders.[20]

The meeting to nominate candidates for the county election was another tumultuous affair, with scuffles breaking out between Old Irelanders and supporters of the Tory candidate, William Monsell. There were fist fights on the stairs of the courthouse, and a man was 'thrown out of the gallery' onto the bodies below. Such violence was far from uncommon in elections during the 1830s and 1840s. It was often orchestrated, with mob 'captains' hired by candidates and paid well to create mayhem. Rank-and-file rioters would also be given a few shillings for their services. The mobs of Cork and Limerick had particularly notorious reputations.[21] When order was eventually restored, Sir David Roche, the county sheriff, asked for nominations. John Dowling, a solicitor from Newcastle West, came forward, but was shouted down by Old Irelanders. Persevering, he nominated Smith O'Brien. Matthew O'Flaherty from Croom seconded the nomination. Smith O'Brien, Dowling admitted, had no knowledge of his name being put forward. A 'large section of the electors', however, had determined not to lose his valuable services. Dowling yelled out 'Repeal and no compromise', a slogan of Smith O'Brien's, and said the Young Ireland leader would always be preferred 'as long as place and pension are not preferred to patriotism'. This was met with cries that Smith O'Brien was a 'Tory' and after 'Castle money'. Three more candidates were nominated: Monsell, Powell and a second Old Irelander, George John O'Connell. The commotion was so intense that the sheriff had to plead with the crowd to push back as 'the gentlemen of the press' were being 'crushed to death' and could not take notes.

The county elections took place over the course of several days, from 11 to 14 August. This was more than a week after the voting in the city, elections at this time not always running concurrently. It was clear from early on that the poll would be headed by Monsell, who had undertaken an extensive canvass. The fight for the second seat was a straight contest between Young and Old Ireland, the *Reporter* delighting that 'without preparation … without a canvass, without organisation, without money, without his presence, or even his knowledge', Smith O'Brien looked to be edging ahead of Powell. Smith O'Brien's name and years of service had clearly won him many ardent supporters. His votes, however, came in the main from electors living west of the River Maigue. This was Smith O'Brien's home territory and the *Reporter* praised the people of west Limerick for standing so ably by their 'beloved' representative.[22]

Smith O'Brien, an aristocrat and a Protestant, transcended these labels to win support from a broad range of the community. He had the backing of middle-class electors such as Dowling, as well as landlords like John Fitzgerald, one of the Knights of Glin. William Griffin, his physician and confidant, also assured Smith O'Brien that 'all the R.C. Clergy of the Diocese of Limerick with two or three exceptions are anxious for your nomination and will give you their support'. Smith O'Brien's backing, however, spread far beyond those endowed with the vote: as an assiduous and conscientious MP involved in many local issues, he had earned the affection of the ordinary people of west Limerick, who boycotted the O'Connellite *Pilot* in 1846 when it turned against him.[23]

The conclusion of the election was as unruly as its commencement. The candidates – bar Smith O'Brien – and their supporters gathered at the courthouse on the evening of Saturday 14 August. Monsell (588 votes) and Smith O'Brien (482) were declared the winners by the sheriff, who then needed soldiers to keep order. John O'Donnell – a solicitor in Limerick city who had helped organise Smith O'Brien's last-minute campaign – tried to say something on his behalf, but could not be heard. Smith O'Brien's supporters were heckled on their way out of the meeting and had to be accompanied into the city by a 'troop of Dragoons', with 'turf and several stones' being thrown at them. They repaired to O'Donnell's house at 9 William Street, where the soldiers spent two hours holding back a mob.[24]

John O'Donnell, the twenty-nine-year-old co-founder of the *Limerick and Clare Examiner*, was an archetypal Young Irelander. His first meeting with Smith O'Brien had been during the summer of 1846. The *Examiner* had changed hands in the meantime and O'Donnell had become more involved in Young Ireland. He made his first appearance at the Irish Confederation in June 1847, warning the Irish people that if they continued to elect place-hunters, they would 'deserve to remain the creatures they are, despised and trodden on, without strength or courage to turn on their oppressors'. He had been asked to work as an election agent for other candidates, including Powell and Monsell, but had refused, working instead for Smith O'Brien without payment.

Daniel Doyle was a local solicitor who also worked on Smith O'Brien's campaign. He received a letter of thanks from Smith O'Brien (as did O'Donnell and John McClenahan), which he said he would hold on to forever in the hope 'that at some future time, I may render myself in some degree worthy of the good opinion so flatteringly expressed in it'.[25]

A hyperbolic *Reporter* proclaimed Smith O'Brien's win

the 'greatest triumph ever recorded in the history of elections'. John Dowling delighted in recounting how 'without a canvass, without preparation, organisation, or money' they had 'appealed to the virtue of the constituency and in the face of the most violent intimidation, returned you to Parliament'. A letter from Newcastle West described exultant Young Irelanders lighting bonfires in celebration, and putting up a large flag bearing the name of Smith O'Brien. A few bitter Old Irelanders removed the flag, but were caught and given a 'good drubbing'.[26]

Smith O'Brien returned to Limerick on Saturday 28 August, just a day before supporters from all over the county – from Newcastle West, Rathkeale, Adare, Croom and Askeaton – descended on his home in Cahirmoyle. Some had travelled by foot, whilst others came in jaunting cars. They entered through a 'majestically wooded demesne' and congregated by a temporary platform erected on an 'imposing eminence' to the south-west of Cahirmoyle House. Bands played music before Smith O'Brien appeared on the stage, praising his audience as proven old allies and 'hard workers … in the cause of truth and nationality'. Congratulatory addresses were read out by the deputations, many of them linking Smith O'Brien with his great ancestor Brian Boru, or 'Brian the Brave'. There were also cheers for McClenahan and the *Reporter*, 'the only independent Repeal Paper in the South', and for Richard O'Gorman and the 'gallant 37 of Limerick' who had voted for him. When the majority of the crowd had departed, Smith O'Brien retired to his home. A number of local people stayed behind, however, 'delighting themselves on the green with music and the merry dance'. They did not leave Cahirmoyle until late in the evening, when it was dark and bonfires had been lit 'on the surrounding hills, to commemorate the happy reunion of the tried and true Smith O'Brien with his Constituents'.[27] Smith O'Brien had united all strands of west Limerick opinion behind his banner; the goal of Young Ireland – never to be achieved – was to replicate that success nationwide.

'THE GOOD WORK IS FAIRLY BEGUN'

William Smith O'Brien's Limerick triumph aside, the 1847 general election was a disaster for the Young Irelanders. Having been cowed into fielding only a few candidates, their efforts to win pledges against place-hunting had been far from successful. The return of almost forty Conciliation Hall repealers, meanwhile, gave the impression that John O'Connell and the Repeal Association would continue to dominate nationalist politics in Ireland. The *Nation* admitted there were grounds for 'mortification'.[28]

The scale of the failure compelled the Young Irelanders to drastically remodel their movement. Attention was turned to the establishment of a network of confederate clubs around the country. These clubs, it was hoped, would boost the profile of the Irish Confederation. Duffy even imagined them staging events to commemorate local heroes: confederates in Limerick, he suggested, could hold a soirée 'on the birth day of [Patrick]

Sarsfield', the great defender of Limerick during the sieges of 1690 and 1691.[29] The clubs, which were both political and educational, would be quite autonomous – in sharp contrast to the highly centralised Repeal Association. Another factor informing the inauguration of the clubs was the security they could provide for confederate gatherings now regularly disturbed by Old Irelanders. In Dublin in mid-July, for example, a crowd of Old Irelanders had spent an evening chanting the name of O'Connell outside a Young Ireland event. When the Young Irelanders eventually spilled out of the meeting, the two sides engaged in running street battles, during which Thomas Meagher and a number of others were knocked down and trampled upon. Richard O'Gorman senior – one of the treasurers of the confederation and a man in his sixties – was hit on the head with a stick on Sackville Street (now O'Connell Street). The police needed reinforcements to quell the trouble.[30]

The Sarsfield Club in Limerick, one of the first confederate clubs to be formed outside of Dublin, grew out of a meeting in John McClenahan's house on Anne Street. The other founding members of the club included Daniel Doyle, Fr John Kenyon, and William and Daniel Griffin. The Griffins, both doctors, were older brothers of the recently deceased Limerick novelist Gerald Griffin, author of *The Collegians*. William Griffin especially, had been a close friend of Smith O'Brien's since the early 1830s. McClenahan's letter to Smith O'Brien informing him of the meeting said simply: 'The good work is fairly begun. May God prosper it.'[31]

The first official meeting of the Sarsfield Club was held on Saturday 11 September 1847. Its success, according to McClenahan, exceeded all expectations 'both as to money, members and enthusiasm'. The editor was particularly enthused by the fact that a lot of trade unions in the city, 'who were supposed to be all Old Irelanders', had shown an interest in joining up.[32] At a second meeting, held two days later, Smith O'Brien – who was not present – was elected president of the club. Fr Kenyon and Alderman Michael Dawson were made the vice-presidents, with Alderman William O'Hara as treasurer and John O'Donnell as secretary. Kenyon spoke of how the 'grand aim' of the club 'was to elevate the people by improving their minds' so that they might 'have the skill to free themselves from the yoke of the oppressor'. The club would hold lectures and have a library, and its rooms would stay open until late at night so that members could read newspapers and discuss issues of significance. Daniel Griffin, who was quite a conservative figure, then explained how a great sense of 'dissatisfaction' with Conciliation Hall had left him and many other repealers with little choice other than to join the confederation 'or take no part in forwarding the great question which involved the freedom and happiness of the country'.

The leaders of the Sarsfield Club, mirroring the movement as a whole, were predominantly middle-class professionals. However, the number of tradesmen involved in Limerick city is also important. The Richmond Ward Club, a tradesmans' club which included among its membership the blacksmiths

Thomas Ahern and Charles O'Neill, dissolved to join the Sarsfield Club en masse. The union representing cabinet makers in the city also indicated an intention to join up. The Sarsfield Club may have been run by the middle classes, but it was not their domain entirely.[33]

Doyle – acting secretary while O'Donnell was away on business in London – described to Smith O'Brien how busy he had been 'collecting subscriptions, attending committees and writing letters to those persons I thought likely to join the Club'. The club had also taken permanent rooms at 51 William Street, not far from Todd's, the well-known department store. It already had 'over eighty members', with subscriptions amounting to more than £16. The records of the confederation provide details of these subscriptions: leading figures, such as O'Hara and Daniel Griffin, paid £1 each, while others contributed anything between one and ten shillings. The records also show that, a few weeks later, thirty-four members of the Guild of Cabinet Makers sent a total of about seventy shillings up to the Irish Confederation headquarters in Dublin – an average of two shillings each.[34] Doyle asked for membership cards to be sent down.

Smith O'Brien accepted 'with pride' the position of president of the Sarsfield Club. Duffy wrote to him hoping that 'Rathkeale and many other localities in your neighbourhood' would follow the example of the city. They did, and the *Limerick Reporter* soon carried news of a confederate club being formed in Newcastle West. The club, the writer perceived, would be 'an important boon' to the people of 'a country town like this' during 'the long winter evenings', with talented speakers such as Smith O'Brien and Tom Meagher expected to travel down and give talks. The Brian Boru Club, established a few weeks later in Rathkeale, was a bit more forceful in its language; Patrick O'Dea, one of its leaders, stated: 'We start here early next week, in God's name, and in open, undisguised contempt to all humbuggers.'[35]

Twenty confederate clubs had been formed by the end of October, including eight in England. The clubs in England – springing up among the Irish populations of Liverpool, Bradford and London – were an important part of the Young Ireland movement, not least for the vital funds they sent over. The confederates in England drew a lot of support from, and were closely aligned with, the Chartists, whose leading figure was an Irishman named Feargus O'Connor. The Chartists were an opposition movement built around the six points of the People's Charter of 1838, which included the demand for universal male suffrage and the secret ballot. O'Connor had a history of disputes with the Liberator, and John O'Connell wasted little time in painting the Young Irelanders as radical 'Chartists and Traitors'. Some Young Irelanders themselves were uncomfortable with the close ties, including Richard O'Gorman junior, who feared that the 'very violent spirit of Chartism' manifesting itself in some of the working-class clubs in Dublin 'would divert the people from Irish business and make them Englishmen in their politics'.[36]

The Young Irelanders were buoyed by the early success of the club movement, despite some reservations about the increasing influence of Chartists. The good mood was added to by the clear deterioration in the popularity of the Repeal Association during the autumn of 1847, its funds drying up and its MPs disunited in parliament. The Young Irelanders found succour, too, from events on the Continent, where the liberal-minded Pope Pius IX was relaxing censorship laws and freeing political prisoners in Rome.[37] The election of 'Pio Nono' was seen as a boon to liberals and nationalists throughout Europe, not just in the collection of kingdoms, duchies and statelets that made up Italy. The confederates hoped his leadership would make the clergy in Ireland – still closely entwined with Conciliation Hall – more amenable to their cause.

The renewed confidence of the Young Irelanders found expression in the desire of clubs to hold large public meetings. Meagher, on a tour of Munster, was in 'high spirits', writing to John Mitchel of how the 'star' of the confederation was 'rising' in both Waterford and Cork. The Sarsfield Club, gaining a number of prominent adherents – including W.H. de Massy, a wealthy County Limerick landlord and magistrate – began to prepare for a big event of its own. O'Donnell, discussing the club's plans with Smith O'Brien – who would be the main speaker – suggested an afternoon start to avoid trouble with Old Irelanders, who had just sabotaged a similar meeting in Cork. O'Donnell had conferred with the working-class members of the club and told Smith O'Brien they were happy 'to sacrifice one half day' of work (and pay) to attend.[38]

The Sarsfield Club meeting was organised for the Theatre Royal in Henry Street on Wednesday 20 October. The Limerick confederates hoped at first to have Meagher on the platform alongside Smith O'Brien. The young orator, however, was unable to attend and Richard O'Gorman was sent down in his place. O'Gorman was invited to stay at Cahirmoyle, and wrote a letter to Smith O'Brien saying that he would be there 'wind, weather and the Board of Works permitting'. As the two Young Irelanders dined at William Griffin's house the night before the event, O'Gorman was given a copy of the motion he was to read, and wished only that he 'could do it full justice – a Denunciation of the association of Old Ireland is called for'.[39] William Griffin held talks with the police, and an advertisement for the meeting relayed how all precautions had been taken to preserve order. However, not even a plea from an Old Ireland priest in the city to let the confederates 'have their meeting in peace' could stop opponents from congregating outside the theatre at noon. Those attending the meeting ran through a gauntlet of hooting Old Irelanders. The hall, with a capacity of almost 2,000, was nevertheless close to full, a separate gallery housing the ladies present. Tickets had been a shilling each, though free for Sarsfield Club members, now numbering over 200. Smith O'Brien was among the last to arrive; those accompanying him kicked on their way into the building.[40]

A heavy rain soon dampened the spirit of the Old Ire-landers, and they dispersed. Smith O'Brien, taking his place on the stage, spoke of the Famine, Patrick Sarsfield and Pius IX. He praised the 'valour' and 'courage' of the people of Limerick, insisting nonetheless that the time was not right for any 'appeal to arms'. The confederates, he declared – with a clear view to winning over the landed gentry – were 'friends of social order'. They would achieve repeal through the influencing of public opinion and other legal means. O'Gorman, William Griffin and many more speakers followed him onto the stage.

The meeting lasted several hours, and it was dry and dark by the time it ended. The Old Irelanders had reassembled and threw dirt and other missiles at Smith O'Brien – a man they had helped carry through the streets a year earlier. Patrick O'Dea from Rathkeale was 'kicked' to the ground and struck 'with a stone on the back'. His friend Stephen Hayes was hit on the forehead, severely cut and 'robbed of his hat'. Charles O'Neill, a Young Irelander, produced a 'brace of pistols', the sight of which sent the rioters running and yelling through the streets 'like a tribe of wild Indians, insulting and assaulting everyone they met'. In the days that followed, a number of the rioters were arrested and brought before court. One man was fined £1, whilst others were let off after expressing remorse. The disturbance, however, had worked – from an Old Ireland perspective, at least: the Sarsfield Club did not get the fresh influx of members it had hoped for, a fact confirmed in a letter from Griffin to Smith O'Brien a few weeks later.[41]

THE 'GREATEST REFORMER OF THE AGE'

Throughout the autumn of 1847 the columns of the *Limerick Reporter* carried news of dramatic happenings in Italy. The *Reporter* condemned the Austrian government's decision to send extra troops to its garrisons in the Papal States as a provocative gesture aimed at cowing the liberal pontiff. It praised Pope Pius IX as the 'greatest reformer of the age', and revelled in the idea of a conflict in Italy proving the 'harbinger of independence' to every nation struggling under the 'withering curse of imperialism'. Local news gave less cause for optimism. A threatening notice – signed 'Molly Maguire' – put up around Famine-racked Clare warned against the transferring of corn out of the county. A week later, a horse was shot dead as it carried corn into Limerick market.[42]

The harvest of 1847 was the healthiest since the beginning of the Famine. The extremely weak state of the peasantry, however, meant considerably fewer potatoes than usual had been planted. The amount of food available for consumption remained dangerously low and the *Reporter* prophesied 'the same starvation as last year and worse'. Attacks on landlords and their agents also continued, and on the morning of Thursday 18 November a 'great alarm' spread through Limerick city following the murder of a land agent named Ralph Hill. Hill, from Clare Street in Limerick, was shot from behind a hedge belonging to a farmer named Quane, from Roxboro on the outskirts of the city. Hill had gone there to oversee the collection of corn for his employer. English newspapers, such as *The Times*, made a great noise about these murders of landlords and agents. The *Reporter* compared such aggrieved declamations with the virtual silence that greeted 'the victims of extermination, who have perished silently by the ditch side, or from fever in the workhouse'.[43]

The main response of the re-elected Whig government to the unrelenting Famine in Ireland was a coercion bill designed to stem the spate of attacks, burglaries and murders sweeping the country. Sir George Grey, the home secretary, introduced the bill to parliament in late November, impressing upon MPs its necessity in light of figures that showed a dramatic increase in serious crimes such as murder, attempted murder and the stealing of arms. The home secretary highlighted Limerick as one of three counties – with Tipperary and Clare – accounting for more than seventy per cent of these crimes. J.J. Kennedy, a police inspector in west Limerick, would have welcomed the new bill that allowed for the disarming of proclaimed districts in Ireland. He had appealed for such a change in the law a few weeks earlier. The *Reporter*, however, denounced the government for pursuing coercive measures rather than providing for 'a perishing population'.[44]

A number of Repeal Association MPs, frightened at the growing levels of agrarian crime, supported the coercion bill, thereby splitting John O'Connell's parliamentary party in two. The bill provoked rifts in the Young Ireland ranks also, with John Mitchel particularly forceful in his opposition. Mitchel, horrified by the worsening conditions of the

Famine, had come under the influence of James Fintan Lalor, a powerful writer whose objective was *'to repeal the Conquest, – not any particular part or portion but the whole and entire conquest of seven hundred years – a thing much more easily done than to repeal the Union'*. Mitchel – soaking up Lalor's radical ideas about tenant rights, peasant proprietorship, rent strikes and physical resistance to evictions – began to stray from the Young Ireland line, and informed Smith O'Brien how 'my doctrine is nearly identical with Lalor's'.[45]

The increasingly hostile tone to Mitchel's writings caused disputes with those more moderate Young Irelanders who did not wish to alienate the landed gentry from the movement. Duffy even censored some of the more incendiary pieces that hinted at a national insurrection. Relations between the pair deteriorated to such an extent that Mitchel resigned from the *Nation* in early December. Such conflicts in the offices of the *Nation* – the beating heart of the Young Ireland movement – carried over quite naturally into the Irish Confederation. The Young Irelanders, it was clear, were starting to split between the moderates – intent on pursuing constitutional means of opposition – and the militants, such as Lalor, who wanted 'a prepared, organised, ordered, orderly, and *resistless* revolution'.[46]

The Crime and Outrage (Ireland) Act – commonly re-ferred to as the Coercion Act – was passed by parliament in late December. The Repeal Association was in disarray, but the Young Irelanders, fighting among themselves, were in no position to take advantage. Everything, it seemed, was crumbling beneath the heavy weight of the Famine. Limerick was among the first counties to be proclaimed, and preparations were made to collect weapons. The posters announcing the proclamation went up quickly across the county. It was, the *Reporter* opined, 'an appropriate Christmas Box to Ireland from the Whigs'.[47]

3

'TIMES OF STORM
AND UNREST'

A dense, cold fog shrouded the streets of Limerick city on the night of Tuesday 11 January 1848. But the poor weather failed to dampen the chorus of approval that met William Smith O'Brien, the Young Ireland leader, as he entered the William Street rooms of the Sarsfield Club, of which he was president. The loud, hometown cheers that greeted his arrival were greatly heartening, as recent months had proved most trying. In November a trip to Belfast had left him bloodied and bruised, 'the dregs of the Old Ireland Repeal party' disrupting several meetings there.[1] A journey to parliament in December had proved similarly futile, the Coercion Act passing easily into law. Smith O'Brien's opposition had been hindered both by a heavy flu and the servility of fellow Irish members.

Smith O'Brien had returned to Ireland in mid-December, travelling home to Cahirmoyle in west Limerick. Dejected and ill, he refrained from full engagement with the arguments breaking out between the Young Irelanders in Dublin, the increasingly radical John Mitchel animated particularly by clauses in the Coercion Act that allowed for the disarming of proclaimed districts. Mitchel's outlook on the Famine had hardened considerably during the last months of 1847, and he wanted to refashion the Young Ireland movement – with its emphasis on constitutional methods of opposition – into something decidedly more dangerous. An alarmed Charles Gavan Duffy had kept Smith O'Brien informed of the new thrust to Mitchel's views, including his threats to the government about 'secret societies'.[2]

When the initial clamour in the Sarsfield Club died down, John O'Donnell, the secretary, read out a 'most cheering' statement of its progress, prospects and finances. Smith O'Brien returned to centre stage and explained how all the confederate clubs in Ireland, numbering just eighteen at the time, were having their affairs looked into. He perused the Sarsfield Club's account and minute books, and declared them satisfactory. The club's library, he continued, contained a 'very choice and excellent collection', and he was glad to see 'French and Irish classes already formed, and several other classes in [a] state of formation'. He expounded on his own deep knowledge of the Irish language and advised those students present to 'apply themselves to the examination of old Irish manuscripts'. He praised the quality of the lectures being delivered by members but encouraged that still more be given, one of the great principles of the Irish Confederation – the political wing of the Young Ireland movement – being the elevation of the character of the country. He stressed that the speakers should not be confined to the more educated members of the club as even the 'humblest mechanic among them could tell them something about his own trade which they did not know'.[3]

Libraries and lectures – the beneficent power of education – were vital elements of the confederation ethos. Nevertheless, it was to a sustained chorus of 'hear hears' that Smith O'Brien switched focus to remind his audience that 'the primary object' of the confederate clubs was not 'an instructional but a political one'. He had 'read with sorrow' a recent letter of Mitchel's to the *Nation* arguing for the replacement of 'stupid' legal agitation with the 'deliberate study of the theory and practice of guerrilla warfare'. The relinquishing of arms under the terms of the Coercion Act, Mitchel warned, would be tantamount to 'virtual suicide'. Smith O'Brien, still wedded to constitutional means of opposition, told the meeting he could 'not concur in the policy or sentiments' the letter propounded. The club members decided to discuss the matter more fully at a later meeting and the night closed with Smith O'Brien promising to donate some recently published Irish books, and the announcement that Brian Dowling, a merchant, would soon deliver the first in a series of lectures on the American revolution.[4]

During the course of the Sarsfield Club meeting, Smith O'Brien had remarked that although the political strength of the confederates 'was not great at present', it did not follow that this would always be the case.[5] He was optimistic because the hold on the country of Old Ireland appeared to be waning, its facile opposition to the Coercion Act much commented upon. Some Old Irelanders in Limerick, appalled at the discreditable scenes in parliament, had turned their minds to the idea of reunion. A small delegation led by the cooper Jeremiah Forrest arranged a visit with Smith O'Brien a few days prior to the meeting of the Sarsfield Club. Smith O'Brien had welcomed them warmly into the home of his father-in-law, Joseph Gabbett, at 78 George Street (now O'Connell Street). He saw little hope of reconciliation, however. It was the Old Irelanders, he stated bluntly, who had 'got rid of us' before allying with 'the liberal government that let our people starve'.[6] Reunion, it seemed, was a long way off.

THE 'TRODDEN WORM MAY TURN AT LAST'

William Smith O'Brien did not attend the first anniversary meeting of the Irish Confederation, held at the Round Room of the Rotunda in Dublin on the evening of 12 January 1848. The event passed off without serious incident, but tensions were clearly rising, with latent divisions being brought to the fore by the callous Coercion Act. The majority of the leadership – foremost among them Duffy and Smith O'Brien – remained attached to the dual idea of constitutional action and class unity. They recoiled from any precipitate move towards violence, believing it untenable in a country ravaged by ongoing famine. The more extreme views of Mitchel, gaining prominence especially among the proletarian members of the Dublin clubs, advocated civil disobedience, the arming of the people and non-payment of rents.

Mitchel had already severed his connections with the *Nation* to set up a new newspaper of his own, the hugely popular *United Irishman*, which had been 'established specifically as an Organ of Revolution'.[7] The prospectus of the *United Irishman* was printed in the *Limerick Reporter* on 1 February 1848. That same issue carried the news of an insurrection in Sicily, the island off the south-west coast of Italy that was linked to the Bourbon dynasty of Naples and ruled by the despotic Ferdinand II. Parallels with Ireland were swiftly drawn. The *Reporter*, edited by the Young Ireland-supporting John McClenahan, stated:

> Sicily, in its natural and political history and in its social conditions, presents strong points of resemblance to Ireland, and the present throwing off of the Neapolitan yoke is pregnant with warning and instruction to England and her rulers, that the tyranny practised over the Irish people may one day become intolerable, and what has happened once in Sicily may happen again in Ireland. Let British statesmen, legislatures and politicians, be warned that if they persist in misgoverning this unhappy country, the trodden worm may turn at last, and despite all the efforts of the friends of peace, the standard of revolt, aye, and of successful revolt may be raised, and the natural ally of England ... be forever lost to her.[8]

McClenahan's hopes were short-lived. The Sicilian rebellion was quickly overshadowed by more discord within Young Ireland, an anxious Richard O'Gorman describing to Smith O'Brien how 'wearied and disgusted' he was 'with our squabbling here'.[9] Smith O'Brien, with characteristic stubbornness, paid no heed to the calls of Duffy, O'Gorman and others to return to Dublin as soon as possible. He had political duties to perform in Limerick and also wished to spend some time with his wife Lucy and their six children. He was, however, gravely concerned that Mitchel's writings were damaging the confederation and, in particular, his hopes of co-opting more Protestant landlords to the Young Ireland cause.

When he finally travelled up to the capital in late January, Smith O'Brien acted decisively, presenting to a general meeting of the Irish Confederation ten resolutions that in essence reiterated the basic principles of legal agitation and the combination of classes – meaning an alliance with landlords. The ensuing debate, generally cordial, lasted a wearying three days. Smith O'Brien, a landlord himself, praised Mitchel personally, but argued that arming the people in the present adverse circumstances – famine and a lack of great popular support – would lead only to 'confusion, anarchy and bloodshed'. Mitchel, for his part, did not call for any immediate uprising but insisted on the need to arm the people. He also made clear his antipathy for the majority of Irish landlords, stating he would not waste any more time trying to accommodate them into the Young Ireland cause. A vote late on the third night of the meeting upheld Smith O'Brien's resolutions. A few days later, Mitchel, Thomas Devin Reilly and John Martin resigned from the council of the confederation, though not from the confederation itself.[10]

The difficulties for Young Ireland were compounded in late February by the defeat of Thomas Francis Meagher in a Waterford by-election. The cause of this election was the acceptance by Daniel O'Connell junior – one of the Liberator's sons – of a consular position in France. This episode reaffirmed confederate complaints about Repeal Association place-hunting, and the running of the young and charismatic Meagher for a seat in his native Waterford was a brief source of excitement. Two members of the Sarsfield Club, Daniel Doyle and William Lane Joynt, even travelled there to assist Meagher in his campaigning. In the event, however, Meagher came third and last in the vote, behind the Whig Sir Henry Winston Barron and the Old Irelander Patrick Costelloe. Smith O'Brien made another dispiriting journey across to parliament soon after this failure, labelling the other Irish members in the House of Commons 'tame as well beaten hounds' who 'licked the hand which struck them'.[11] In this atmosphere of torpor and dissension, the news of revolution in France struck like lightning.

'GLORY TO THE FRENCH PEOPLE!'

Brought to the throne by the July Revolution of 1830, King Louis Philippe, the 'Citizen King', was undeserving of the appellation, with corruption and economic crisis the chief traits of his regime. A reform rally scheduled for 22 February 1848 was cancelled at the last minute, but Parisians took to the streets regardless, and were soon joined in cries of 'Down with the ministry' by disgruntled members of the National Guard. 'Men endowed with a kind of frenetic eloquence' harangued 'the populace at street corners', whilst others 'were in the churches ringing the tocsin as loudly as ever they could'. The demonstrations went on for more than two days, and as lead was cast for bullets and cartridges were rolled, the trees on the boulevards together with benches, urinals and railings were put into service as defences. 'Paris,' wrote Flaubert, 'was covered with barricades.'[12]

Louis Philippe dismissed his prime minister, François Guizot, but on the streets behind the barricades, power passed from the reformers to the radicals. On the night of 23 February a small knot of protesters, red flag in hand, clashed with a contingent of troops on the Rue de Capucines. Shots were fired and a score of protesters left dead. A funeral procession formed, more barricades were raised, and riot turned ineluctably to revolution. On 24 February Louis Philippe abdicated, and a provisional government was established, consisting in the main of well-known reformers such as Alphonse de Lamartine, but including also more radical figures like Louis Blanc as well as the symbolic ordinary worker, Albert. That night, the Second Republic was proclaimed from a balcony of the Hotel de Ville.

'Glory to the French people!' exulted the *Limerick Reporter*. 'They are worthy of liberty. Their noble deeds kindle holy emotion and sympathy in every breast not dead to the pulsations of freedom.' The monarchs of Europe were 'quaking on their thrones', and the time had come for England to 'give us back our parliament, at once, and let every man have his own country'. For all of Europe, the revolution in France carried a great deal more weight than any outbreak in Sicily. The members of the Sarsfield Club, like other confederates across the country, drafted congratulatory addresses to the French people. They also put candles in all the windows of the club on Sunday 5 March, and flew 'a large and beautiful Tricolour Flag, and beside it the Green Flag of Ireland, trimmed with white, and both having golden tassels'. John O'Donnell, recently elected onto the council of the Irish Confederation, suggested the best way of showing support for France was 'by cherishing the like unquenchable hatred of tyranny' and 'by exhibiting ... the same intense devotion as that which prompted the Citizens of Paris, in defence of their rights, to oppose their naked breasts to the sabre and the musket' and in three short days 'hurl the hoary despot from his guilty eminence (hear, hear, and loud cheers)'.[13]

The following day, 'a grand and universal illumination' took place in Rathkeale in west Limerick in support of the French revolution. 'The whole town lighted at an early hour' with tar barrels 'blazing at various points', shots 'fired in all directions', and with 'bands playing spirit-stirring national airs'. Cheers were heard for the *United Irishman*, and a soldier who helped light a bonfire outside Magee's public house was arrested and confined to his barracks.[14]

According to the *Reporter*: 'Nothing could exceed the excitement and joy of the people of this city upon the arrival of the news of the complete triumph of Young France over hoary despotism.' The Limerick magistrates, however, held quite a different view. Joseph Tabuteau sent Thomas Redington, the under-secretary of state for Ireland, a poster acclaiming the French revolution that had been put up around the city. He acknowledged some people in Limerick were disposed 'to create disturbance' but had 'no reason at present to believe it will succeed'. Tabuteau wrote again on the evening of the Sarsfield Club's illumination, stating that, as of five o'clock, there had not been 'the slightest attempt at a meeting, and the town wears the appearance of an ordinary Sunday'. The Young Irelanders, he continued, had 'exhibited three flags from the windows of their Club room, one of which is the Tri-Coloured flag, but the circumstance has not created the slightest interest and not a soul has stopped to view them'.[15]

The people of Limerick had perhaps more vital issues on their mind: food and shelter. The four major workhouses in the county were all dangerously overcrowded, and it was about this time that three young girls, Bridget Hayes, Honorah Downey and Bridget Clune, so dismayed at the dire conditions in which they lived, fled the auxiliary workhouse at Mount Kennet in the city while still wearing their flimsy workhouse clothes. They were quickly caught and jailed for stealing workhouse property – their ragged workhouse clothes. The *Nation* also carried reports of how coffins had become scarce in Limerick city so great was the demand. 'The dead', it concluded morbidly, 'will soon have to bury the dead.'[16]

Despite the unruffled view of Tabuteau, the temper of Irish nationalism was transformed by events in Paris. Revolution, it was felt immediately, was on the march, Irish minds recalling easily the centuries of past affinities with France. One of the members of the new provisional government in Paris, Alexandre Ledru Rollin, had even attended Daniel O'Connell's monster meeting at Tara in 1843. In Cork, Joseph Brennan, an eloquent but impulsive young confederate, shocked even members of his own Desmond Club when he proclaimed – after the mayor had refused to call a congratulatory meeting for the French people – that Ireland had 'a surplus of landlords and fat aldermen', and that 'blood was a commodity of which there would soon be lavish expenditure'. Lord Clarendon, the lord lieutenant of Ireland, trembled 'to think of the amount of disaster that may be oncoming ... The lower orders in Dublin are already somewhat excited and say now that the French have got their liberties they will come and help us get "repale" [*sic*]'.[17]

In Dublin, Alfred Webb, a printer's apprentice just fourteen years old, described how he and his friends 'were profoundly moved by the Revolutionary events of 1848'. They concocted plans over lunch 'for the throwing up of barricades', and 'promised at all events to stand firmly by each other when we found ourselves in the dock'. Webb, later a prominent Home Ruler, even put together a little biography of John Mitchel, 'then my special hero'. Another young man with a large future in Irish politics, the Fenian John O'Leary, recalled in later years how it 'was well to be young then', when minds 'were in a state of constant ferment' and bodies rushed about 'from one club or meeting to another'.[18]

For the Young Irelander O'Gorman, events were 'hurrying so fast' that no man could say 'what treasures lie hid in the depth of tomorrow'. The sense of exhilaration was so great, even moderate Young Irelanders began to speak out in a manner that made a mockery of earlier criticisms of Mitchel, who was by now even 'more Jacobin than the French' according to Duffy. An ebullient Tom Meagher declared himself 'in raptures', wanting '*bold strokes*, and nothing else!' Duffy, meanwhile, urged the formation of an armed national guard, and together with John Blake Dillon discussed the procurement of 'funds and military aid from our countrymen in America', contemplating rebellion once the harvest was collected. The Young Irelanders were also impressed by the significant role played in events by journalists in Paris, Lyons and elsewhere.[19]

This burst of zeal and fervour was dampened slightly by fears that the Mitchelite wing (and the Dublin clubs especially) could carry the country too soon down the path to open rebellion. Mitchel's mindset in the aftermath of the French revolution is clear from passages in his *Jail Journal* that argue 'depopulated, starved, cowed and corrupted' as Ireland was, still it was better to 'attempt resistance, however heavy the odds against success', better 'that men should perish by the bayonets of the enemy than by their laws'. Smith O'Brien – who hailed the French revolution and was heartened by its largely bloodless nature – still viewed any immediate outbreak in Ireland in terms of 'rashness' and 'criminal folly'. He also still wanted more input into the Young Ireland movement from the higher orders of society – the landlords and gentry Mitchel rebuked. Class unity was his goal, but with leadership coming unquestionably from the men of property, the upper and middle classes. Duffy, likewise, feared 'a mere democratic' rising 'which the English Govt will extinguish in blood; or if by a miracle it succeeds ... will mean death and exile to the middle, as well as the upper classes'.[20]

'GOD CALLS FOR UNION'

At the meeting of the Sarsfield Club on the night of the illumination, John O'Donnell spoke of his 'sincere and unaffected pleasure' at seeing so many Old Irelanders present, accepting it 'as a happy omen – as the harbinger of returning brotherhood amongst Irishmen'. He hoped that night's proceedings marked 'the commencement of our renewed union' and that 'all our paltry and unmeaning differences' would be 'obliterated and forgotten'. In a letter to Smith O'Brien a few days later, he described the meeting as 'densely thronged by men of all parties' exhibiting a 'most anxious desire for reamalgamation'.

The following afternoon, in another show of harmony, members of the Sarsfield Club and the trade unions (staunch Old Irelanders in the main) met and marched together with bands and banners to the spacious corn market that even with 'the wetness of the day … was completely filled'. The new mayor, Michael Quin – an O'Connellite said by O'Donnell to be 'in disfavour for his lukewarm sympathy to the late French doings' – attended the meeting, albeit briefly. Another congratulatory address was drafted to the French people before the majority of the crowd dispersed to cries of 'Vive la République'. Those who stayed on listened to preposterous schemes to raise 200,000 soldiers to send to France in case any despot, such as Tsar Nicholas I, interfered with the young republic.[21]

Reconciliation was also on the minds of the Young Ireland leaders, 'unity' and 'fraternity' the fresh bywords. Conciliatory articles appeared in the *Nation* and *Pilot* newspapers, erstwhile antagonists. Smith O'Brien – fearful that the myriad divisions within Irish nationalism would see a great opportunity for strong action go to waste – initiated talks with the Old Irelanders in Dublin. One of the first signs of a thaw in relations was a meeting of the Irish Confederation at the Music Hall in Dublin on 15 March 1848, where 'the coal porters, formerly so hostile to the Confederation, had volunteered to act as wards-men for the evening, a duty freely entrusted to them, and most faithfully discharged'.[22]

The signs of reconciliation in Ireland were aided by a fresh torrent of news from Europe, where Viennese democrats, Czech moderates and Hungarian aristocrats were striking blows against the heart and periphery of the vast and sprawling Austrian Empire. The *Nation* thrilled at reports of riots convulsing the streets of Milan and Venice, and of constitutions being won by liberals in many states of the German Confederation, including Baden, Nassau, Württemberg and Bavaria, where the unpopular King Ludwig had a Limerick-born mistress in the dancer Lola Montez. 'Times of storm and unrest', observed a character in Thomas Mann's *Buddenbrooks*.[23]

'Land after land', the *Nation* declared, had 'thundered for its rights' and the rulers had all 'trembled and obeyed'. The forces of conservatism, however, had not given up power without struggle – often terrible. The Habsburg general, Joseph Radetzky, after five days of horrific street fighting, ordered one last destructive bombardment of the city of Milan before retreating north. The battle for Berlin on 18 March, meanwhile, was among the most ferocious of the year, with troops attacking barricades with cannons, 'frightful hand-to-hand fighting' and houses 'overcrowded with dead and wounded'. The streets 'swam with blood' before King Frederick William of Prussia finally relented to his citizen's demands for a constitution.[24]

The intoxicating wave of rebellion sweeping through Europe was not enough to obliterate local enmities in Ireland. In Limerick, a number of meetings were held between the Young and Old Irelanders in an attempt to organise a demonstration for St Patrick's Day. Difficulties arose over a joint petition the two groups were drafting. The Old Irelanders wanted it sent to parliament, but this was against the principles of the confederates, who did not recognise Westminster's power over Ireland. The Sarsfield Club wished instead to address Queen Victoria, and was supported in this stance by a leading article in the clearly partisan *Limerick Reporter* that pointed out how both Daniel and John O'Connell had petitioned the queen many times in the past. O'Donnell raised new issues, too, making clear his displeasure with some of the ingratiating wording suggested, such as 'respectful gratitude', which, he said, made him want to cut off his hand.[25]

John Pigot, a barrister and Young Irelander based in Dublin, was dispatched to Limerick to take part in the negotiations. On Thursday 16 March he reported back to Smith O'Brien on the final meeting between the parties. The Sarsfield Club delegation had consisted, in part, of Pigot, O'Donnell, William Griffin and John McClenahan of the *Reporter*. The group of Old Irelanders included the mayor, Revd Dr O'Brien of St Mary's parish, James McCarthy of the *Limerick and Clare Examiner*, and a few trade unionists. Once more, the Old Irelanders, following instructions from Dublin, advocated a petition to parliament that the Young Irelanders rejected. 'At last it fell from Dr O'Brien that the forms having been sent *from Concn* [*sic*] *Hall*, they were reluctant to depart in one word from them.' One agitated Old Irelander then threatened 'that such violence & riot never was seen in Limerick as would take place if we did not adopt a petition to Parliament'. The meeting broke up soon after this outburst. The Revd Dr O'Brien, however, 'expressed a hope' that the 'conference need not terminate without taking some steps towards a future union'. He suggested they form 'a common club to read out the news from France & Italy, if they could agree on no more'.[26]

St Patrick's Day passed off peacefully in Limerick even though the army had prepared for disorder, occupying the city at strategic points with 'cannon pointed from the barracks' and 'provisions and rum laid in for a siege'. Three days later, on Monday 20 March, the Old Irelanders, heeding at last the strong mood for reunion, gave way on their earlier preconditions. A joint committee of Young and Old Irelanders sent a public letter to the mayor asking him to convene a 'Meeting of the inhabitants of this City, on Saturday next, the 25th of March, at two o'clock for the purpose of adopting an address, respectfully calling upon the Queen to take measures for the re-assembly of the Irish Parliament'. Ten men from each side were to take charge of the preparations.[27] In response to this new accord between the repealers of Limerick, the sheriff, Henry Maunsell, sent Lord Clarendon an 'Address from the City of Limerick' signed by more than 200 members of the gentry and business elite. They pledged, in view of 'the lamentable state of agitation which surrounds us', their 'unalterable attachment to our Sovereign and to the institutions over which she presides'. The signatories included the businessmen William Roche, William Spaight and Edward Hartigan, the architect James Pain and the founder of Barrington's Hospital,

Matthew Barrington.[28] Their clear message was that Limerick remained loyal.

The army was in full view once again on the morning of Saturday 25 March. Though acting provocatively, according to the *Reporter*, 'it was in vain that scouts of huzzars were galloping to and fro, and keeping a sharp lookout for the enemy with their forests of pikes from the plains of the county of Limerick, and the mountains of Clare and Tipperary!' In the early afternoon, members of the various trade unions – the coopers, carpenters and coach builders, the slaters, sawyers and stonecutters, the plasterers and painters, shipwrights, millwrights and nailers – gathered in the rain on Clare Street to unfurl their large flags and colourful banners. They walked a circuitous route through the city, led off by the bands of the temperance societies and cheered all along the way. They crossed Mathew Bridge and, to strains of 'The Glories of Brian the Brave', converged on the potato market on the banks of the River Shannon. 'Not only was the entire area of the market densely filled, but the railings, the roofs of the sheds, the windows of the large houses in front, and the pathways outside.' The *Reporter* made an exaggerated claim of some 10,000 people being present. The conservative *Limerick Chronicle* put the figure closer to 3,000 – a sizeable number all the same.[29]

The mayor, Michael Quin, spoke first, lauding the sight of the union between Old and Young Irelanders. The Revd Dr O'Brien – an Old Irelander – followed him onto the podium and said of past difficulties: 'We disagreed in the desert, only because we loved the promised land so much.' He continued on the theme of union, declaiming provocatively: 'the graves of the famine dead and the cabins of the famine-stricken call for union'. He concluded with a cry of 'God calls for union', while at the same time and to loud cheers taking the hand of John Corbett, a well-known grocer belonging to the Sarsfield Club. Among the many later speakers were a number of ordinary labourers, followed by Daniel Doyle reading aloud the address to be sent to the queen demanding the restoration of a native Irish parliament.[30]

A 'NEW INCENTIVE TO HATE'

William Smith O'Brien, John Mitchel and Thomas Francis Meagher had been arrested for sedition a few days before the mass meeting in Limerick. Placards went up around the city announcing an urgent meeting at the Sarsfield Club. John O'Donnell asserted that he was not 'alarmed or cast down' by the arrests, but that every 'fresh insult was a new incentive to hate'. John Dowling, a solicitor from Newcastle West, read out amidst cheers a resolution that pledged those present 'to sustain our illustrious President [Smith O'Brien] with our fortunes, and if necessary with our lives in his struggle for the independence of this land'.[31]

The charges against Mitchel related to inflammatory articles he had recently published in the *United Irishman*. Smith

O'Brien and Meagher were indicted for speeches they had made at a meeting of the Irish Confederation in the Music Hall in Dublin in mid-March. The apparent – though, in the end, illusory – success of the revolutions across Europe combined with the ineffectiveness of his latest efforts in parliament had led Smith O'Brien to speak out in a manner far stronger than heretofore. Smith O'Brien had begun with familiar phrases about the need to exhaust legal means of opposition, warning that any immediate insurrection would be 'put down in a week'. He then changed direction, explaining how he was no longer against 'intelligent young men' turning their minds to military matters and 'guerrilla warfare'. He called for the formation of an armed national guard and spoke openly of a French invasion of Ireland, military aid from America and the mutiny of Irish soldiers in the British army. He also admitted for the first time to being 'miserably disappointed' with the inaction of his fellow landlords, warning that they faced having their lands 'sold as national property' in the aftermath of any national struggle.[32]

Smith O'Brien saw the prosecutions as a deliberate government ploy to taint the confederation with the militant *United Irishman* views. Nevertheless, in a show of solidarity and strength, the three men had walked together to police headquarters in Dublin on the morning of Wednesday 22 March. Surrounded by supporters, they followed a course from the committee rooms of the Irish Confederation at D'Olier Street up through College Green and Dame Street. John O'Connell, likewise showing support, offered bail for Meagher and Smith

O'Brien. Afterwards, the three 'Prosecuted Patriots' returned to D'Olier Street to deliver speeches. Richard O'Gorman also spoke, declaring to great cheers: 'Although as yet I have not had the honour of receiving the attention of the Government, I'll give them cause soon to pay me a visit.'[33]

A delegation of Young Irelanders led by Smith O'Brien left for France not long after the three 'Prosecuted Patriots' were bailed. Their purpose was to present a number of congratulatory addresses to the new government in Paris. In this respect, they mimicked nationalist movements across the continent. The expedition, however, was unfulfilling, as the new French leader, the poet-politician Alphonse de Lamartine – retreating from an earlier radical foreign policy manifesto – offered only vague expressions of support. The most significant result of the journey was the presentation of a tricolour flag to Meagher – the green, white and orange representing the union of Catholics in the south with Protestants in the north; this, he brought back to Ireland as a new national emblem. Nevertheless, the ratcheting up of political tension continued unabated. Smith O'Brien spoke to the United Ireland Club in Paris about the need for all supporters of Irish nationalism to familiarise themselves with arms, and from the end of March the spectre of pikes and rifle clubs began to dominate communications between the Limerick magistrates and Dublin Castle.

When the first murmurs of confederate arming reached Pierce George Barron, the Limerick magistrate was calm in his response, advising Dublin Castle that he had made inquiries but found no proof for the rumour that 'one of the Wardens of the Confederate Club here, was extensively engaged in making Pikes'. He did, however, note a 'very inflammatory & seditious placard ... posted this morning through the City, signed "Michael Doheny".' It carried the name of a Dublin printer and he promised to send a copy for investigation. Barron, a Catholic from Waterford, had moved to Limerick in the summer of 1847 after several years as a magistrate in Mayo. According to the *Castlebar Constitution*, he was a man of 'uniform mildness, suavity and uprightness' who would be greatly missed by the gentry of Mayo.[34] Barron might not yet have been overly concerned about the confederates in Limerick. That did not stop him regretting Limerick city had not been proclaimed at the same time as the county, as the 'persons who have not got Licences in the Counties of Clare & Limerick place their arms with their friends in this City, ready to receive them when required'. Limerick city, he feared, could be a 'great focus of organisation' in the event of any disturbance. The Sarsfield Club, nevertheless, was 'well watched', and 'up to this period their proceedings have produced no sympathy or excitement among the mass of the population'.

The mass of the people were probably too debilitated by the Famine – the month of April witnessing the forced migration of 150 women from Limerick to Australia in an attempt to ease the unconscionable numbers living inside workhouses.[35] The political temperature, nonetheless, grew increasingly febrile throughout Limerick during April. Newspapers carried stories of pikes being brought into the city in coffins – complete with weeping widows alongside – while Barron heard of pike heads 'deposited at the confederate Club Room' for the price of '2s 6d each'. Rifle clubs, too, became more prominent, with parties of Young Irelanders going 'openly about the Town with their rifles on their Shoulders'. The confederates had started to practise 'in the Quarries in the neighbourhood of the Town daily and till a late hour at night'. With the city not yet proclaimed, there was little the police could do to stop such actions. Elsewhere, Dublin confederates held weekend rifle practice and shooting competitions in the Wicklow Mountains, while similar activities took place in Cork, Waterford, Galway and Kilkenny. These rifle clubs helped attract greater numbers into the orbit of the confederate cause, the comradely element attractive to young men who might not have held strong political views. In Limerick, young women were occasionally present at the rifle practice – another reason to join up and show off one's prowess.[36]

The *Limerick Reporter*, naturally, was full of information on the 'two or three rifle clubs being got up in this city'. It advised readers on the price and availability of firearms in Limerick, how 'a first-rate single gun (twist barrel)' could be had at Mara's 'for about two guineas', and a rifle for seven or eight pounds. One article described rifle club members meeting 'at the Quarry, on North Strand, for practice, and their shooting, which we had the pleasure of witnessing, was admirable. Even with "smooth bores" some of them hit the bull's eye several times at a distance of eighty yards.' The target some of the clubs used was a picture of Clarendon.[37] Another article in the *Reporter* described how a 'few of the soldiery' sent to watch the practice 'took part in the amusement, and made some tolerable shots, but by no means to be compared with the close hits of the civilians'. 'Perhaps', the writer speculated, 'they wanted to show how they could miss a mark when they wished.' This insinuation that Irish soldiers in the British army would refuse to turn their weapons on their own people reflected a popularly held view of the time – a view encouraged by the example of the National Guard in Paris, and promulgated even, by Smith O'Brien. For Mitchel: 'The soldiers of several regiments, being Irish, were well known to be very willing to fraternise with the people upon a first success, and the police, in such an event, would have been a green-coated Irish army upon the moment.'[38]

The *Reporter*, increasingly daring, was soon reprinting articles from the *United Irishman* entitled 'Our War Department' that described how best to drill and make gunpowder. Other columns carried rumours of huge shipments of pikes coming into the port of Dublin from Liverpool. The United Repeal Club of Limerick was formed – though, in truth, the two sides never truly conjoined – and at a meeting of the Sarsfield Club, in reply to an excited cry from the floor that the Milanese had their archbishop leading them in the fight against Austria, the Revd Dr O'Connor declared: 'Yes, and you will have the Priests with you should the time ever come that you want them to lead you.' In Rathkeale, the nearest large town to Smith O'Brien's Cahirmoyle estate, rifle practice was said to be held every evening, despite the county being proclaimed, and the people were 'in high pluck and spirits'. There were even drawings 'of Pikes and improved Pitchforks' on the doors of several houses. The ideal pike would have a 9-foot handle of seasoned ash and a 12-inch spear.[39]

A 'VERY DISLOYAL AND SEDITIOUS FEELING'

In response to the ever-bolder Young Ireland behaviour in Limerick, James Sexton of Richmond Place – a former sheriff – sought Lord Clarendon's 'sanction in forming a volunteer force to be ready to act if any consequences should require it'. A priest called Evans, from Kilmallock in east Limerick, noted a 'very disloyal and seditious feeling' spread among his parishioners. Publications such as the *United Irishman* were being exhibited in shop windows to deleterious effect, argued Evans, providing details of a letter some men in the local workhouse had drafted for Mitchel's newspaper. The letter stated that 150 of them in the workhouse were 'able and willing to take the Pike or Gun and rush forward as soon as the word of command is given'. The writers promised to extract themselves 'from the yoke of Misrule and Tyranny which is the cause of having so many stout Hearts thrown into a Poor House to be fed with the refuse of Slaves in other countries'.[40] The British government was to blame for their penurious circumstances, these men believed, and they were willing to take retaliatory action. Evans had obtained his copy of the letter through an informant, William Gavin, one of the paupers from the workhouse.

Clarendon did not take up Sexton's offer of a volunteer force, but there was growing concern among his subordinates in Limerick. Barron now definitely wanted the city to be proclaimed, as being 'placed in the centre of proclaimed districts … it affords a ready & safe depository for the Arms of those who would not be allowed to carry them in any of the adjoining districts'. The topic of 'special constables' arose, and Barron thought 'it would be most desirable to have such a body sworn in', warning that their selection 'should not be left to the Mayor of Limerick, an avowed Repealer'.[41]

Barron may have been alarmed by the striking appearance on the night of Monday 27 March of a great number of fires atop the mountains of Tipperary, Limerick and Clare. This vast illumination of the countryside, each fire going up in response to the other, was caused by the mistaken belief it was 'a signal of rejoicing for some victory achieved by the disaffected in Dublin'. The cause, however, of the first fire that gave signal to all the others was more mundane: the burning in Murroe of 'a craggy field of furze'.[42] It was, nevertheless, an ominous sign of the enthusiasm that would greet any move against the government.

Police spies set to work, and in early April two men claiming to come from Bruff purchased pikes at Thomas Ahern's Vulcan

Iron Works at 13 Catherine Street. Ahern, a member of the Sarsfield Club, was suspicious of the men, named later as Kelly and Riordan. His son followed them and watched them report back to a police station. The two men had visited other black-smiths in the city to gather information, even though it was still legal to buy and sell pikes. For the *Reporter*, these under-hand methods were an attempt to frighten the blacksmiths. But rather than be cowed, Ahern was emboldened, and promised to exhibit a pike head in his window. It was reported later that 'one of the wretches that bought the pikes at Mr Ahern's shop came back afterwards. Mr Ahern was not at home; but Mrs Ahern denounced him, a crowd collected, and would have stoned him to death had he not fled for his life.' It was also rumoured that a detective 'assuming the character of a Frenchman' had been visiting the Sarsfield Club. 'The people have their eye upon him,' the *Reporter* warned, 'he is not safe in Limerick.'[43]

The confederates in Limerick were full of confidence by the end of April, and made plans to hold soirées for the three 'Prosecuted Patriots'. Joseph Tabuteau wrote to Dublin of the need for efficient government note-takers to be present at these events – planned for the city and Rathkeale – as it was likely the three Young Ireland leaders would 'express their senti-ments freely'. Proper records would be needed for any future prosecutions, and while the police might be able to take down 'particular sentences sufficiently accurate' and 'furnish the general purpose of the speeches … a regular Government reporter on the spot … could furnish the long words' and 'support the police in the general sense they take of the meaning of the speeches'. No such person was available in Limerick, but a note attached to this letter read: 'W. Hodges & his son both excellent reporters will arrive at Limerick on Friday night and attend the meeting there & at Rathkeale for the purpose of taking notes of the speeches delivered.'[44] The Limerick soirée, however – ostensibly a celebration of the three leaders – was to take a startlingly unforeseen course.

4

THE 'ATTACK ON THE LIFE OF MR MITCHEL'

William Smith O'Brien stopped off in Limerick city on the evening of Saturday 22 April 1848, the day after Good Friday. Accompanied by his wife Lucy, he had travelled down on the day coach from Dublin, a journey of some ten and a half hours involving a train ride to Roscrea and horse-drawn carriage through Tipperary. Word of his presence spread quickly and a crowd gathered outside the Sarsfield Club in anticipation of an address. This was Smith O'Brien's first visit to Limerick since his arrest with Thomas Francis Meagher and John Mitchel – arrests that had seen the Sarsfield Club establish a fund for the three 'Prosecuted Patriots', with £16 raised on the first night. A similar fund had been set up by the parish priest in Adare, Fr O'Grady, who spoke to his congregation on the matter one Sunday morning and who contributed an impressive £5 of his own money.[1] In the period since his arrest, Smith O'Brien had been to Paris, and on the way back made what would prove to be his final appearance in the House of Commons. His journey from

Dublin was to combine a visit home to Cahirmoyle with a tour of the confederate clubs of Munster, where the formation of a national guard would be discussed.

Smith O'Brien was reposing at the home of his father-in-law Joseph Gabbett, when he was approached by Dr Daniel Griffin of the Sarsfield Club to make a public oration. Smith O'Brien insisted at first that he was too tired to speak after the journey down. He ultimately consented, however, and was led by a band to the club rooms, where tar barrels blazed out front and a large tricolour flew high from a window – the new flag of green, white and orange brought back from Paris by the Young Irelanders to signify union between the Catholics of the south and Protestants of the north. Close to 1,000 people were waiting for Smith O'Brien outside the Sarsfield Club, and they erupted into cries of 'Brian Boru' when they saw him approach. Smith O'Brien spoke to the crowd from a second-floor window, still urging caution but nonetheless allowing for the possibility of violence when declaring that the issue of repeal would soon be resolved 'one way or the other', and that the Irish nation 'would vindicate itself even in the last extremity'.[2]

The stirring reception for Smith O'Brien in Limerick city was matched a few days later in Rathkeale, when 'even the busy season did not prevent the hardy sons of toil from flinging aside their implements of husbandry' to help form a procession in the town to greet their leader. There were cries of 'Vive la République' and 'Welcome home from Paris of the

Barricades'. Patrick O'Dea, the secretary of the local confederate club, the Brian Boru Club, read out a congratulatory
address. Smith O'Brien then took a stroll through the town,
and was 'saluted from the windows and house tops by rounds
of cheers, and waving of handkerchiefs, which this noble
patriot courteously returned, frequently uncovering his head,
and bowing as he passed along'.[3] It was hoped and expected
that these euphoric scenes would be outdone the following
Saturday when Limerick was to hold a soirée for the three
'Prosecuted Patriots', Smith O'Brien, Meagher and Mitchel.

The soirée, according to its advertisement, was being held
by the 'United Repealers of Limerick'. In truth, it had been
organised by the Sarsfield Club, and it was simply using the
term 'United Repealers' to portray inclusiveness and to reflect
the support it had received. It proved an unfortunate choice
of wording, as a letter appeared in the *Limerick and Clare
Examiner* from the Revd Dr O'Brien of St Mary's parish, dis-
puting its validity and stating the committee of the United
Repealers of Limerick had not even met to discuss the event.
Importantly, and showing his opposition was not just a case of
semantics, the Revd Dr O'Brien also mentioned recent articles
from Mitchel's *United Irishman* that labelled Daniel O'Connell
– his shadow still looming large over the city – 'an abetter of
English plunderers'. The priest demanded that 'O'Connell's
Memory' be removed from the list of the night's toasts; he did
not want it tainted by the presence of Mitchel. In response to
these concerns, two prominent members of the Sarsfield Club

– John O'Donnell and Daniel Doyle – inserted a letter in the *Limerick Reporter* that stated the committee referred to by Revd Dr O'Brien no longer existed, and had, they believed, been wound up with the staging of the 25 March meeting. They also argued that the degree of cooperation they had received from the trade unions in Limerick justified their use of the moniker 'United Repealers'. The complaints regarding Mitchel's increasingly divisive writings were harder to get around. They insisted, however, that he was a patriot deserving of support even if one dissented from some of his opinions.[4]

Revd Dr O'Brien – who lived at 65 Nicholas Street near King John's Castle – was relatively new to Limerick city, having worked previously in Nova Scotia, where he said he had been an advocate of repeal.[5] He became an important figure very quickly, however, and although an O'Connellite, had approached Charles Gavan Duffy earlier in the year regarding 'union of the parties'.[6] He was on the committee of the Limerick Society for the Promotion of Literary, Scientific and Industrial Education with a number of Young Irelanders, and even attended a meeting of the Sarsfield Club in early April, speaking out in a spirited fashion on the success of the Lombardians against the far better equipped Austrian army.[7] Nevertheless, the cause of reconciliation between the repealers of Limerick was not far enough advanced to assuage his fury over Mitchel's calumnies against O'Connell, the great Liberator. He printed off copies of his letter, and distributed them as handbills around the poorer areas of Limerick, stoking up the anger of O'Connell's numerous supporters in the city – men for whom his name was almost holy. Limerick's long history of faction-fighting was about to gain yet another inglorious chapter.

'DEATH TO MITCHEL'

The day of the soirée, Saturday 29 April, began inauspiciously, with Mitchel and Meagher – who had travelled down together on the overnight mail coach from Dublin – confronted immediately by a sullen crowd of Old Irelanders. Shouts of abuse were hurled at them until a number of confederates intervened and ushered the two visitors to the safety of Cruise's Hotel. Smith O'Brien – who had been at home in Cahirmoyle – arrived in the city a few hours later, quite wary on account of the presence of Mitchel. He had been surprised and disappointed by Mitchel's acceptance of the invitation to the Limerick soirée as this seemed to contravene an earlier agreement the two men had reached. According to an early biographer, however, Mitchel viewed the Limerick soirée – held explicitly for the three prosecuted Young Irelanders – as quite separate to Smith O'Brien's wider Munster tour, and 'did not understand that he was precluded in honour from accepting a particular invitation such as this by his consent to not accompany Smith O'Brien on his southern tour'.[8]

The setting for the soirée – the lower floor of a recently vacated brush factory at 42 Thomas Street – was the organisers' second choice of venue. They had been refused permission to use the Theatre Royal on Henry Street because of purported threats made to the owner by the military. Tickets for the event were two shillings apiece, and the spacious room – a hundred feet long – was 'decorated with evergreens' and 'brilliantly illuminated with gas'. A reasonable crowd of about 300 attended, including the government reporter William Hodges. The ladies present were seated in a separate gallery, and the stewards wore rosettes of green, white and orange on their coats. Tea and refreshments were served – prepared by Mr Lennon, a local hotelier – whilst the orchestra was made up of the St Mary's Volunteer Repeal Band. The red-and-yellow coat of arms of the O'Brien family hung proudly above the centre of the stage, together with the family motto, *Lamh Laidir an Uachtar* (strongest hand uppermost). A number of people stayed away, however, on account of the threats and intimidation of a crowd of mostly lower-class working men who had gathered outside the soirée from the early evening.[9]

Daniel Griffin – flanked by Mitchel, Meagher and Smith O'Brien – began the official part of the meeting at 7.30 p.m. However, according to Smith O'Brien's own account:

> Scarcely had the proceedings of the evening commenced when the groaning of the O'Connellite mob assembled outside the building was followed by the throwing of stones. Before long an attempt was made to set fire to the house by burning an effigy of Mitchel close to the window, and a regular battery was established against the

door. After the proceedings continued (under the eyes of
the police) for more than half an hour, the door was at
length broken to pieces.

Smith O'Brien wanted to go outside and talk to the raucous
crowd. He was restrained by friends, and it was only when the
burning effigy of Mitchel was flung through an upstairs window
that he spied an opening and at last made it outdoors, stick in
hand, 'expecting to receive a blow immediately upon my issuing
from the opening'. Finding a clearing amidst the chaos of the
crowd, Smith O'Brien flung aside his 'small deal stick', and cried
out 'A cheer for Repeal', hoping the sight of him would prove
calming in all the tumult. He was, instead, punched solidly in
the face. Several people rushed immediately to his aid, calling
out 'Do not injure Mr O'Brien'. They threw their arms around
him to stop him from falling, and whilst 'in this attitude (one of
my arms being raised), I received a very severe blow in my side,
which incapacitated me from any further active exertion'. Smith
O'Brien was carried away from the mêlée, 'and after washing
the blood from my face at the house of a shopkeeper, received no
further molestation on my way to the house of Mr Gabbett'.[10]

The *Limerick Reporter*, not surprisingly, was resounding
in its support of Smith O'Brien and damning of the Old
Ireland mob. Its correspondent explained how, as letters of
apology from a number of local priests were being read out at
the soirée – Saturday-night services making it impossible for
them to attend – a scuffle was heard outside the door, and a

volley of stones was hurled through the windows of the old brush factory. Those inside the hall were not overly concerned at first, the *Reporter* stated, as it was presumed that with the police headquarters and mayor's residence both located nearby, nothing untoward would be permitted to occur. These expectations, however, were to be disappointed.

The assault on the hall continued for almost an hour. The windows were broken and replaced with boards; one of those leading this task, John Corbett, did so 'at great risk to himself and not without receiving some blows'. The original assailants had by this stage linked up with an even larger mob – one that had spent the day fixing up flags with slogans like 'Death to Mitchel'. Primed 'with strong drink', they carried the flags and effigy through the streets. Although men were to the fore, a number of women were involved, too – their aprons overflowing with sharp stones. A few pistol shots were fired at the effigy and into the air as the procession wound its way through the streets of Boherbuoy before arriving at the brush factory. Makeshift battering rams were put together and charged against the door.

The burning effigy of Mitchel – adorned with the inscription 'Mitchel, the calumniator of O'Connell' – was thrown at last into the building. Those inside the hall – armed with a few pistols and the legs of tables and chairs – took this as a signal to open the door and bring the fight to the mob. O'Donnell, Doyle and McClenahan were all seen in the midst of the fighting. Shots were fired on both sides, but when one of the rioters took a bullet in the thigh, it 'was the signal for [the] flight of the entire mob!' The riot quickly petered out, though a few skirmishes and fist fights continued to break out on side streets. It was only at this stage, complained the *Reporter*, that the mayor made his long-awaited appearance, 'as if for the rescue of the mob!' Even more galling, he actually arrested Corbett of the Sarsfield Club, 'who was laudably engaged in preserving the peace that his worship was sworn to preserve, and paid for preserving, but did not preserve!' Once the streets had cleared, the police entered the fray, though again belatedly, 'either to share the victory, or protect their friends … the prominent leaders of the attack on the life of Mr Mitchel'.[11]

The soirée reconvened, though without Smith O'Brien. Meagher, Mitchel and others made vigorous speeches. Afterwards, as Meagher was making his way back to Cruise's Hotel, a stone was thrown at him from the darkness. The missile missed its target and hit instead the hotel owner, a 'lean, eager-looking little man of forty'. At seven o'clock the following morning, Meagher left for Cork for a number of engagements, including a dinner at the Imperial Hotel on the South Mall. Mitchel – who had slept the night at the house of a friend – took the day coach back to Dublin. A subdued Smith O'Brien did not leave for Dublin until that evening, travelling up on the mail coach. His original intention of visiting Cork and Waterford had been overtaken by the need to appear in court on Monday morning in connection with his forthcoming trial. At about the same time as he took his leave of Limerick, some 'juvenile Conciliation Repealers', in imitation of their elders, burned another effigy of Mitchel 'at the May eve bonfires' in the city.[12]

A 'CIVIL WAR OF OPINION'

The aftermath of the riot in Limerick was an unseemly, unedifying affair, a shrill cacophony of claim and counter-claim, of slur and rebuke. One obvious issue to be debated was the culpability of Revd Dr O'Brien, particularly in light of the handbill he had distributed in the poorer parts of the city. Mitchel, apologising to the reconvened soirée for having been the cause of the disruption, was met with a loud chorus of 'no, no, it was Father O'Brien did it all'. From Cork, a few days after the riot, Meagher described how the 'most desperate indignation exists here, in every mind, against the Revd Dr O'Brien and all his ruffians. They would kill him, in spite of his surplice, if he was to be found here.'[13]

A letter to the *Reporter*, from the Revd Dr O'Connor of St Munchin's College, condemned the 'dictatorial arrogance' of Revd Dr O'Brien, 'which would assume to act and speak for the city'. The riot the priest had fomented, O'Connor bitterly complained, served only to show up Ireland to Europe and America, and prove 'how unworthy we are of their sympathy and support in the cause of freedom, when the first blood that was spilt was the blood of the noblest of Patriots, Smith O'Brien'. A similar outlook reigned in the Sarsfield Club, where Daniel Griffin denounced the Revd Dr O'Brien's handbill and other attempts to sow disunion between the repealers of Limerick at a time when such 'disunion must be fatal to the hopes of the country'. He had, he concluded, 'no hesitation in saying Dr O'Brien is not an honest Repealer'. Griffin's words were applauded and echoed throughout the meeting, John O'Donnell admitting that, as a devout Roman Catholic, it anguished him to accuse the Revd Dr O'Brien of being the 'principal instigator' of the riot.[14]

The Revd Dr O'Brien had actually been absent from Limerick on the night of the riot, preaching at the Magdalen asylum in Cork. He returned to the city on Monday evening, 'and was received by a lot of his friends, who apprehended violence to the Rev. gentleman from the Sarsfield Confederates'. He wrote immediately a number of letters in his own defence, lamenting the excesses of the night and avowing that, had he been present, he 'should have jeopardised [his own] life to save Smith O'Brien from personal injury'. But he also hit out at the Young Irelanders of Limerick and their 'very pitiful' efforts to associate him with the riot. He added scornfully: 'They imagined that they led the public mind of Limerick – they have been undeceived, and are angry at their disappointment.'[15]

The war of words between the clergyman and the Sarsfield Club continued apace, an incensed O'Donnell declaring:

If you come in for some hard blows you cannot blame me. The contest is not of my seeking: you were the first to

fling down the gauntlet – I take it up. You have declared
your determination and ability to extinguish the Sarsfield
Club. I, as an individual member of that Club, defy you to
make good your threat on me.

Dr Daniel Griffin – a fairly conservative and highly respected
figure employed by the local poor law union – claimed that,
while speaking to the St Francis Temperance Society on
Athlunkard Street, Revd O'Brien had threatened to return
to America or Canada if his followers did not put down the
Young Irelanders.[16] Other confederates joined in, Bartholomew
Dowling accusing the Revd O'Brien of wanting 'a civil war of
opinion or bludgeons in the city, to establish his dictatorship'.
Dowling, like so many Young Irelanders around the country,
was a young professional with romantic leanings. Aged about
twenty-five, he worked as a clerk with Limerick Corporation,
and contributed ballad poems to the *Nation* that had earned
the regard of Thomas Davis. The Revd O'Brien seems to have
been affected by the hostility towards him and did not appear
at any meetings of the Young Ireland-dominated Limerick
Society for the Promotion of Literary, Scientific and Industrial
Education until August.[17]

The presence of spies and the connivance of the authorities
with the perpetrators of the riot were other major points of
discussion. William Smith O'Brien's recollections make
it clear that he believed the authorities had been less than
diligent in their duties. The *Reporter* shared these sentiments:

'Time was given for the perpetration of that crime, and when the attempt failed, then the civil and military power interfered with a flourish of trumpets.' The *Reporter* went on to observe how, earlier in the day, 'these ruffians were seen drinking at several low public houses – fellows who had not the price of their breakfast'. 'Where did they get the money for the whiskey?' the newspaper asked. 'Secret service money' was its own answer. The calculation behind the government's conceit, the *Reporter* believed, was Lord Clarendon's desire to disarm Limerick city under the terms of the Coercion Act. When this move was announced just days after the riot, the response of the *Reporter* was provocative: 'Let no man who feels the pulsation of freedom in his heart disgrace himself by obeying the enslaving mandate of Lord Clarendon. On the contrary, "now is the day and now is the hour" to manufacture and purchase arms in all directions.'

The mayor, Michael Quin, also came in for some abuse from the Young Irelanders, who saw themselves now as the victims of two coalescing conspiracies: the O'Connellites stirred up by the Revd Dr O'Brien, and government detectives plying the lower orders with drink and the materials of riot. At an animated meeting of the Sarsfield Club two days after the riot, Quin was called 'a well-known reluctant follower' of repeal, who had done nothing for the cause and who had within '30 yards of his door … almost allowed 400 of his fellow citizens, with 200 helpless but heroic women, to be burned alive'. A resolution was passed declaring him unfit for office. According to the *Reporter*: 'It was only when insurance agents seeing a danger of the house being burnt, remonstrated with the Mayor, that his worship consented to take any step to put a stop to this disgraceful riot.' The mayor was stung by these reports, and called into the offices of the *Reporter* at 37 Patrick Street to contradict the impression that he had been slow in quelling the riot.

The articles in the *Reporter* appear exaggerated, and were certainly biased. However, its account of the general events of the night of the riot differs little from reports in the much more conservative *Limerick Chronicle*. The tone and emphasis may vary but the details are essentially the same. Furthermore, the *Reporter* was not blind to fairness and truth on the part of the authorities, and actually praised the magistrate Pierce George Barron for acting 'as soon as he heard of what occurred' by coming down to Thomas Street to restore order.[18]

Of the leading national newspapers, the *Freeman's Journal* – an advocate of union between the repeal factions – agreed that: 'The Attorney-General ... the Saxon parliament in Westminster and the mob in Limerick, seem to act in concert, and most harmoniously do they pull towards the same end.' In an article entitled 'The governmental riot in Limerick', the *Journal* did not doubt the presence of a 'guiding authority', and bemoaned the large network of spies and 'demon emissaries' operating throughout the country whose purpose was to 'create divisions among the friends of the country – to cover with disgrace the cause dearest to Irishmen'. The preoccupation, however, of the

Freeman's Journal – a staunchly Catholic publication – was to defend the Revd Dr O'Brien, of whom it said 'no man could more deeply deplore the occurrence' of the riot.[19] The *Nation* likewise supported the Revd Dr O'Brien, regretting his name had become 'mixed up in that bad business'.

Duffy was far more concerned with William Smith O'Brien's apparent determination in the aftermath of the riot to retire from public life. This would have been calamitous for the Young Irelanders, as unequivocally stated by Duffy in his memoirs: 'No man at that time was so important to the cause.' It was paramount to the movement that any ideas Smith O'Brien harboured of quitting politics be swiftly quashed. Without his leadership, as a Protestant and a landlord, the hopes of the moderate Young Irelanders for an all-class alliance would be certain to founder. The *Nation*'s comments on the riot therefore amounted to little more than a panegyric on Smith O'Brien's efforts for Ireland over the past twenty years. In a remark that later events showed to be open to question, the *Nation* declared Smith O'Brien to be a man 'marked for the time in which he appeared'. Of the riot, like Socrates before him, Smith O'Brien had become a victim of 'native ingratitude'.[20]

The *United Irishman*, even though its owner and editor had been the chief target of the rage at Limerick, focused on compassion for the mob rather than condemnation of the rioters. Mitchel took the opportunity to further his own radical agenda of social change and asked: after being treated like animals for so long, was it surprising that the lower orders of society should act like wild beasts? He did not reproach the authorities in Limerick, but looked, instead, to the absentee landlords who lived off the toil of those forced that Saturday night to such riotous recourse. Slavery, he proclaimed, brought the people to such ends; liberty from the tyrannical English landlords would make them human again. Mitchel was also relatively lenient in his treatment of the Revd Dr O'Brien in the *United Irishman*, despite blaming him for the riot in private correspondence.[21] He was willing to forgo his private convictions in order to promulgate his broader social and political creed.

The riot was a godsend for Lord Clarendon, who was able to both proclaim the city of Limerick and also snigger at William Smith O'Brien's haggard appearance in court two days later: black-eyed and slumped in his seat, he was the picture of a beaten man. The riot also allowed Clarendon to heap scorn on the Young Irelanders through his many newspaper contacts. The *World* – a weekly newspaper he had paid off in Dublin – wrote of the 'tea and treason assemblage in Limerick'. It then compared the 'comical riot' – Irishmen attacking their would-be saviour – with the episode from *Don Quixote* where the unfortunate Knight of La Mancha frees a chain of galley slaves only to see them turn on him and shower him with stones.[22]

The *World* was an invidious newspaper that survived, according to Mitchel, on 'hush-money'. On the advice of his chief secretary, William Somerville, Clarendon had earlier in 1848 made arrangements with its editor, James Birch, on account of the need for a loyalist newspaper to counteract 'the diatribes of the *Nation* and other seditious prints'. Birch – a blackmailer who had served six months in prison – proved an unfortunate choice of ally. In 1850, having already received large sums of money from the secret service fund, he sent Clarendon an invoice for £4,700 for 'suppressing the Irish rebellion'. The fallout from this affair was a court case taken by Birch against Somerville and a very public embarrassment for Clarendon.[23]

Clarendon, an inveterate newspaper intriguer, was also on good terms with John Delane, the young and powerful editor of the London *Times*, and it is due to the manner in which the riot was reported in England that it is still remembered primarily in terms of mockery and farce. *The Times* basked in the 'farce of Repeal', the moral-force Old Irelanders adjudged to have 'reasoned with fists and persuaded with shillelaghs', whilst the physical-force Young Irelanders were reduced to mere 'tea drinkers'. Mitchel and Meagher – 'after thundering threats against the Viceroy and his army' – were said to have 'fled from a few lively Old Irelanders, hid themselves in a pantry, threw their pikes into the housemaid's closet, and dropped the vitriol pot into a dust hole'. The newspaper went on to ridicule William Smith O'Brien through his well-known noble lineage – 'how would Brian Boru have wept over his degenerate descendant' – before concluding: 'the ladies screamed, and that scream was the climax of the Irish rebellion'.[24] The virulently anti-Irish *Punch*, meanwhile, provided the most enduring image of the riot: a sketch depicting an ape-faced Mitchel riding out of Limerick atop a pig-shaped Smith O'Brien, a crowd of pike-wielding 'Moral Force' men behind them, and a weasel-like 'Meagher of the Sword' in flight in the background.

A 'TIE OF PERSONAL AFFECTION'

William Smith O'Brien – returning to something approaching full health and in receipt of numerous deputations and letters of support, including one from the Guild of Carpenters in Limerick sympathising 'with you and your fellow martyrs in the cause of Liberty' – went back on his decision to retire from public life. Furthermore, the riot itself began to assume a new form, the seemingly woeful circumstances turned around and the images of dissension emanating from Limerick acting as a stimulus for reconciliation between the factions. The *Freeman's Journal* called on all repealers to 'unite in love, in sympathy, in co-operation, if we cannot unite in one association'. Formal negotiations between the Irish Confederation and the Repeal Association, cut off in July 1847, recommenced at the offices of the *Freeman's Journal*, with the owner, John Gray, acting as facilitator to the talks. Some semblance of rapprochement with John O'Connell remained important to the Young Irelanders, as the riot in Limerick had shown up the limits of their hold on public opinion outside of Dublin.[25] Certainly, they could not yet hope to match the peerless command of Daniel O'Connell at the peak of his powers.

The *Nation* actually managed to convey another positive slant to the riot, claiming that where, previously, Smith O'Brien's English accent and aloof manner had made it difficult for the ordinary Irishman to connect with him, the indignation provoked by the riot had now supplied a 'tie of personal affection'. Despite the efforts of these oracles of hope, however, the riot in Limerick in many ways proved to be a precursor for the fate that would eventually befall the attempted rising, debilitated as it was by the nefarious work of Dublin Castle spies, the ineffable power of the Catholic clergy, and the fatal divisions between Young and Old Ireland. As the *Limerick Chronicle* succinctly opined in the week following the riot: 'it was treason to Daniel O'Connell and not to their sovereign, that exposed the triumvirate to the summary vengeance of lynch law.'[26]

5

'Prepare, ye Men of '48'

William Smith O'Brien's final appearance in parliament – during the showery evening of Monday 10 April 1848 – coincided with a giant Chartist demonstration at Kennington Common. An aging, iconic Duke of Wellington, charged with defending London from the Chartist masses, complained in the House of Lords of how the meeting had for days placed 'all the inhabitants of the metropolis under alarm, paralysing all trade and business of every description'. The popular novelist Charles Dickens, fresh from the success of *Dombey and Son*, had a more jocular view of proceedings, describing to a friend how he might hoist his 'pennant aboard o' the Chartist Flagship' and 'pour in a broadside on you (in answer to your'n) and rake you fore and aft, you swab'.[1]

The Chartists, like the confederates, had been reinvigorated by the fall of Louis Philippe, and in the thrilling aftermath of Paris, the two bodies had forged an alliance that 'seemed for some weeks to menace the unity of the United Kingdom'. There were lines of difference between the groups, with Smith O'Brien and other Young Irelanders opposed to universal male suffrage. These minor tensions were easily overcome in the euphoria of the 'springtime of the peoples'. In an effort to further the links between the movements, prominent Young Irelanders, including Thomas Francis Meagher and Michael Doheny, made several trips across the Irish Sea, and received rapturous applause from crowds of tens of thousands in Manchester and Oldham around St Patrick's Day.[2]

The morning of the Chartist demonstration found the city of London naturally on edge, previous Chartist rallies – in Glasgow a month earlier, for example – having led to riots and looting. The possibility of political violence – revolution, even – impelled tens of thousands of mainly middle-class citizens to turn out in the rain as 'special constables'; among them was William Gladstone, the up-and-coming Tory politician. With regular troops kept judiciously out of sight, shopkeepers patrolled the streets as government clerks 'laid in muskets and barricaded the windows with official files'. Important buildings, like the Bank of England, were parapeted with sandbags and had 'guns mounted in every aperture'.[3]

The almost 150,000-strong Chartist rally dispersed rather tamely, however, when informed by authorities that a planned march to parliament to deliver a 'monster petition' would not be allowed. The immense gathering on the common – including 5,000 Irish men and women clustered around green flags with the harp insignia – did not spiral into conflagration, and London did not fall to the radicals in the manner of other capitals. Instead, Lord Palmerston, the British foreign secretary, famously dubbed the day 'the Waterloo of peace and order'. John Mitchel believed the whole affair proved the pointlessness of constitutional agitation and urged the Chartists 'never to petition again', and to concentrate instead on taking up arms.[4]

The perceived failure of the Chartist rally emboldened the British government, and in the House of Commons that evening, the home secretary, Sir George Grey, assailed Smith O'Brien in a gratuitous manner. Smith O'Brien, just back from Paris, did not flinch in the face of the insults. With the Chartist leader Feargus O'Connor sitting close by on the opposition benches, he spoke out against the main business of the session, a new bill against Ireland creating the offence of treason-felony. Smith O'Brien, his temper stretched to breaking point, labelled the bill a fresh 'attempt to meet the claims of Ireland by coercion rather than by conciliation'. He raised the daunting spectre of 'a republic in Ireland' before the year was out, and turned positively Mitchelite in his assertion that 'under the present circumstances of all nations, it is the duty of every man to obtain the possession, and to learn the use of arms'. Smith O'Brien's reply to Grey's charge of treason, however, was the most provocative statement of the evening. Denying any feelings of disloyalty to the queen, he nonetheless made clear that 'if it is treason to profess disloyalty to this House, and to the government of Ireland by the Parliament of Great Britain – if that be treason, I avow the treason'.[5]

The treason-felony legislation was aimed directly at the

actions of the Young Irelanders, making it easier for the authorities to prosecute the seditious writings and speeches pouring out of the country since the upheaval in France.[6] The occasional 'hear hears' that accompanied Smith O'Brien's speech against the bill were drowned out by a mass of groans, boos and snide laughter from Whig and Tory MPs. In response to this undignified haranguing, Patrick O'Dea, secretary of the Brian Boru Club in Rathkeale, described to Smith O'Brien how the 'people of this town and surrounding country are exulting with unparalleled joy at the heroic stand which you made on behalf of your suffering Country against the bellowings & howlings of a British beer-garden nicknamed The Seat of Legislative Wisdom'.[7] Smith O'Brien's opposition, however, was futile against so animated and agitated a House of Commons. The bill passed easily through the Commons and Lords, taking its place on the statute book in late April. Its first victim was the firebrand Mitchel.

THE 'MOST HEAVILY POLICED CITY IN THE UNITED KINGDOM'

The events of Monday 15 May 1848, have been called a 'turning point' in the year of revolutions.[8] King Ferdinand II crushed the rebellion in Naples with a display of brutal military force; Parisian radicals stormed the National Assembly and accused the liberal government of having betrayed the hopes of France; Viennese democrats raised the spectre of social revolution and turned the people back toward the arms of their emperor. The fissure between liberals and radicals across Europe had widened dangerously, irreparably. Ordinary people previously buoyed by talk of freedom now feared the onset of anarchy and disorder. Conservative forces sensed an opportunity to reassert their lost authority. Austrian troops regained control on the battlefields of Italy. The counter-revolution had begun.

This shift in mood was less visible in Ireland, where, on Monday 15 May, both William Smith O'Brien and Thomas Meagher were discharged after trials for sedition. The juries, including some Catholics, had been unable to reach guilty verdicts. John Mitchel, however – the third 'Prosecuted Patriot' – was not so fortunate. He was rearrested under the new Treason Felony Act, and saw his jury determinedly packed with anti-repeal Protestants. He went to trial ten days after Smith O'Brien. A swift conviction was secured, and Mitchel was sentenced to fourteen years' transportation. The incendiary *United Irishman* was suppressed.

The news of Smith O'Brien's acquittal saw the Rock of Cashel in Tipperary illuminated with great fires. The reaction in Limerick was more muted. A crowd gathered outside the Sarsfield Club to give three cheers for Smith O'Brien and Meagher, but the confederates held back from obvious cele-brations while Mitchel's fate was still unknown. Daniel Doyle and another member of the Sarsfield Club travelled up to Dublin to visit Mitchel in jail a few days before his trial, reporting back to Limerick on his good spirits. Pierce George

Barron, the local magistrate, also journeyed up to the capital to give evidence at the trial.[9]

At six o'clock on the morning of Friday 26 May – the day after Mitchel's much-anticipated trial – the pensioners of Limerick made their way to the military barracks of the city. This was done 'according to previous orders, news of a conviction of John Mitchel and consequent disturbances, being expected from Dublin by the mail'. Mitchel's conviction, however, spread instead only 'a universal gloom' throughout the city.[10] There was no outbreak of disorder. The elderly of Limerick need not have made their early-morning journey. Several shops in Rathkeale closed their shutters 'as a token of sympathy for the patriot Mitchel'. A 'Mitchel Fund' was also established for the convicted man's family, the members of the Sarsfield Club quickly raising the impressive sum of £50. The response in Limerick was nevertheless much quieter than in Cork, for example, where large numbers marched through the streets chanting slogans until long past midnight. In Dublin, similarly, the great majority of clubs, many of them with hundreds of members, 'were vehemently excited' and, according to Mitchel, believed 'that if an insurrection were to be made at all, it should be tried then and there – that is, in Dublin streets, and on the day of my removal'.[11]

Mitchel approved of a rescue attempt in the capital and hoped it would lead to a spontaneous insurrection across the country. The St Patrick's Club, of which he had been president, was particularly anxious for action. The confederate leadership, however, was against so bold a bid and justifiably wary of the 11,000 troops and 1,100 police that made Dublin the 'most heavily policed city in the United Kingdom'. Meagher and Richard O'Gorman – the latter just returned from a month's training with the National Guard in Paris – went on a tour of the capital's clubs – now numbering more than twenty – and found them 'unprepared, unorganised, unarmed, and incapable of being even roughly disciplined for any military attempt'. Deputations from Cork, Limerick and Waterford also rushed up to talk the clubs out of any rash action.[12]

Smith O'Brien was noticeably silent during the period of Mitchel's trial, retreating at first to a friend's house in Wicklow and then down to Cahirmoyle to his wife and children. In part, he feared his mere presence in Dublin would encourage some reckless rescue bid. In the aftermath of the riot, he had also wanted to make clear again the gap between his political position and Mitchel's. On a more personal level, Smith O'Brien was still recuperating from the attack in Limerick and from the stress of his own trial. Writing to his friend, the poet and landlord Aubrey De Vere, he told how he still suffered 'occasionally from the pain in my side earned by the severe blow which I received'. There were also struggles going on within his own family, where, behind his back, his older brother, Sir Lucius O'Brien – the MP for County Clare – was in contact with Lord Clarendon. During a visit to the family estate at Dromoland, meanwhile, the ailing Smith O'Brien was forced to endure 'a short & most painful interview' with his strongly disapproving mother.[13] Nevertheless, and with all these factors taken into consideration, Smith O'Brien's detached behaviour towards Mitchel still appears as a harsh abandonment of a fellow traveller.

THE MARTYR MITCHEL

'May 27, 1848. – On this day, about four o'clock in the afternoon, I, John Mitchel, was kidnapped, and carried off from Dublin, in chains, as a convicted "Felon".' So begins the famous *Jail Journal*, John Mitchel's coruscating account of his years as a British prisoner first at Bermuda and then Van Diemen's Land (now Tasmania), a convict colony off the south-east coast of Australia. A clear, if fraught, opening for action had been let pass by the Young Ireland leadership. Mitchel's transportation, however, was not the end of their agitation. Enraged by the contemptuous mockery of a fair trial, vast numbers of Irish men and women took to the confederation with great vigour. The number of clubs swelled to more than 200, the ostensible membership reaching almost 40,000. The complexion of the clubs changed also. They became more radical, forged in the image of their new hero, the martyr Mitchel; a police spy in Dublin even reported how the council of the confederation had been charged with cowardice and that the clubs were talking of shaking them off.[14]

In response, the moderate leaders – perhaps fearful of losing the reins of power – became more warlike, too. A small group, including the previously estranged Charles Gavan Duffy and Thomas Devin Reilly, began at last to properly formulate plans for rebellion, and 'for the first time, measures were taken to obtain money, arms, and officers from abroad, to make a diversion in England, and procure the co-operation of the Irish residents there, and to prepare particular local men to expect the event'. Terence Bellew MacManus – a Liverpool-based confederate and childhood friend of Duffy's – promised to 'seize a couple of the largest Irish steamers at Liverpool' and 'load them with ammunition and arms from Chester Castle, where there were supplies for an army'. Martin McDermott – an architect and confederate from Birkenhead near Liverpool – was sent as the Young Ireland envoy to Paris to raise men, money and arms. McDermott had been a member of the earlier delegation to France and his proficiency in French – seen in the poem 'Aux Français' published in the *Nation* – was perhaps part of the reason for his selection. Martin O'Flaherty, a Galway solicitor, and John Mitchel's younger brother William were likewise dispatched to New York. The acknowledged leader of the Young Irelanders, Smith O'Brien, was kept mostly in the dark about these secretive proceedings.[15]

Hopes of assistance from America were particularly high, with an Irish Republican Union (IRU) having been established in New York in March 1848 'to promote revolutions for the establishment of Republican Governments throughout Europe, especially in Ireland'. Encouraged by the cataclysmic events in Paris, the IRU raised money and lobbied American politicians on behalf of 'persecuted Ireland'. It drew up covert plans for military intervention, and began to organise an 'Irish brigade' with special attention paid to the recruitment of battle-hardened Irish-American veterans of the recently ended Mexican War (1846–48). Mitchel's conviction in May gave rise to brief hopes of a rescue attempt in Bermuda. William Mitchel, meanwhile – fast following his brother across the Atlantic – reached New York in late June, a month prior to his fellow envoy O'Flaherty. His subsequent tour of American cities – where he was 'fêted on the streets by processions led by Irish brigades with pikes and tricolours carried proudly aloft' – was, on the surface, extremely successful.[16]

Back in Ireland, the Dublin confederates were particularly vigorous in the organisation of new clubs, establishing a 'cordon of these fortresses of popular power from Ranelagh on the South, to Clontarf on the North'. Cork and Tipperary were likewise galvanised by Mitchel's transportation, leading a disappointed *Reporter* to ask: 'What is Limerick about?' Within a week of this call, however, and in clear homage to Mitchel, the Felon Club was established in Newcastle West, enrolling more than seventy members in just two days, Young and Old Irelanders alike, and with Smith O'Brien as its president. 'Remember Mitchel', the club's motto, was written in large letters on a flag displayed from the club windows. Such names were commonplace in the aftermath of the transportation; Caherciveen in south Kerry, for example was home to one of many clubs 'called by the great man's name'. Edward O'Flaherty, a priest connected with this club, wrote to the *Reporter* praising the 'spirit of nationality' that breathed through its pages. Meanwhile, the man after whom all these clubs had been named was out at sea, on his way to penal servitude in Bermuda, complaining of 'weak eyes' and 'sleepily pouring over [Richard Henry] Dana's "Two Years before the Mast": a pleasant, rough kind of book, but with something too much hauling of ropes and "handling" of sails in it'.[17]

On Sunday 25 June, eighty members of the recently established Felon Club paraded from Newcastle West to Cahirmoyle to visit Smith O'Brien. Following doctor's orders, Smith O'Brien had returned to Cahirmoyle at the start of the month to recover 'his strength and mental equilibrium'. He had not really participated in the fresh impetus given to the Young Ireland movement by Mitchel's transportation; nor was he privy to the full extent of the secret plans being hatched in Dublin by Duffy and others. That night, however, 'in a large field convenient to his mansion', Smith O'Brien warmly welcomed those he termed his 'Brother Felons', and re-engaged forcefully with the agitation. In a rousing speech, he promised to 'combat every evil which operates against my country's independence' and to 'labour as religiously as ever, even unto death, if necessary, in the cause of nationality'. With patriotism now 'deemed a crime', he continued, 'the name of felon has become a virtue'. He thus rejoiced 'at being President of the Felon's Club'. Smith O'Brien concluded by inviting his visitors to enjoy a tour of the 'pleasure grounds' of his estate.[18]

The buoyant mood in Young Ireland circles was depressed by the arrival of grave news from France, where the revolution had failed to cure the ills of mass unemployment. Tensions between the moderate and radical republicans – who had combined so auspiciously, if somewhat accidentally, in February – erupted after the closure of the National Workshops into the carnage of the 'June days', a weekend of bloody fighting on the streets of Paris, with the heaviest artillery in the army ranged against the bodies and barricades of the mainly working-class insurgents. Terrible atrocities were committed on both sides, and by the end of the fighting at least 1,500 workers and almost 900 government troops and militia lay dead.[19] For the workers of Paris, the National Workshops had been a potent symbol of their victory in February. The 'June days', it was immediately clear, were equally symbolic, marking the beginning of the end of the 'springtime of the peoples' and the death of its romantic ideals.

A further disastrous effect of the 'June days' on Young Ireland was the clamour surrounding the death of Monseigneur Affre, the archbishop of Paris, who had a year earlier paid a visit to Daniel O'Connell as he passed through France on his way to Italy. Standing bravely before a barricade and pleading for peace, the archbishop was shot down by a government soldier. His death, however – which occurred on the same day as the Felon Club marched to Cahirmoyle – was placed firmly at the door of the insurgents. It fed into fears of social anarchy and upheaval, and strengthened the position of senior clergy already opposed to the Young Irelanders. Newspaper reports of how in 'the "Women's Club" of Paris, the question of "the existence of the Deity" was recently discussed, and only carried in the affirmative by a majority of two votes' did little to assuage the clergy's concerns. The revolutionaries of Europe were godless creatures and the Young Irelanders were tainted by association. Activist priests such as Fr Kenyon in Tipperary and Fr O'Flaherty in Kerry were both suspended from their duties around this period. Kenyon, however, retained the support of his parishioners, who kept the doors of his chapel 'closed and railed' against his successor for a number of weeks.[20]

Another factor that continued to haunt and threaten the Young Irelanders' hopes of rebellion was the still-famished state of the populace. In Limerick, this was brought vividly to the fore in early July when about a hundred emaciated inmates of the temporary workhouse in Boherbuoy took to the streets 'in consequence of the way in which their stirabout was made, being as thin as gruel'. They confronted the mayor, Michael Quin, but were convinced to return to the workhouse with a promise that their derisory meals would be more substantial in the future.[21] The paupers of Limerick could muster themselves to march for food – just about – but could they march for anything more? Could the vague notion of nationhood impel them as their empty bellies had?

'STRONG FEELINGS OF DISQUIET AND JEALOUSY'

'Political zeal is at a very low ebb here', wrote John O'Donnell to Smith O'Brien in a sobering letter towards the end of June. Early, distressing reports of the fighting in France had filtered across the English Channel and Irish Sea. According to O'Donnell, 'the late unhappy occurrence' at Paris as well as 'the illness of our beloved brother Confederate Doctor W. Griffin' had badly affected the progress of the club. The committee members could 'hardly be got together and Doctor D. Griffin has communicated his intention of withdrawing altogether'. O'Donnell mentioned how a new club, the Brian Boru Club, had just formed at Boherbuoy and 'a few others are in progress of formation'. Nevertheless, there remained 'strong feelings of disquiet and jealousy' between the Young and Old Ireland parties in the city, feelings that would take 'some time to subside'. O'Donnell also added, regretfully, that 'the priests do not as yet evince any desperation to unleash themselves at all'.[22]

William Griffin – after a painful, protracted illness – died a few days later at his house on George Street. His death, combined with the departure of his younger brother Daniel from the Sarsfield Club, were heavy blows to the Limerick confederates. Yet there remained signs of life in the Treaty City, and O'Donnell's pessimism was perhaps not entirely justified. When the Brian Boru Club was formed in Boherbuoy, sixty members 'enrolled on the spot, five-sixths of them Conciliation Hall Repealers'. A few weeks later, the Hugh O'Neill Club was established in Arthur's Quay. James McCarthy – an Old Irelander and editor of the *Limerick and Clare Examiner* – was elected president. Kilmallock in east Limerick and Abbeyfeale in the west also founded new clubs. Officially, these were all called 'United Repealers' clubs. In spirit, however, they were confederate clubs, the transportation of Mitchel pushing the Repeal Association into the shade. The Irish League – the new body set up after tortuous negotiations to unite Young and Old Ireland – existed, but was, according to Duffy, a mere 'stripling'.[23] Young Ireland seemed clearly to be in the ascendancy.

Michael Galway, newly appointed magistrate at Abbeyfeale, followed closely the activities of the Oliver Bond Club there. 'They have obtained possession of an unoccupied house,' he informed the Dublin authorities, 'where they meet every day, and take the "Felon" newspaper.' The *Irish Felon* had been established by John Martin to take the place of his friend Mitchel's *United Irishman*, quickly outstripping its forebear in the militancy of its writings. The *Irish Tribune* – founded by two young Dublin confederates, the medical students Kevin Izod O'Doherty and Richard D'Alton Williams – was similarly radical. The influence of these newspapers was a cause of serious concern to Galway, who was reporting a day later on the arrest of 'a man from Ardagh near Wm. Smith O'Brien MP ... charged with practising Rifle Shooting and Drilling'.[24]

Another correspondent with the authorities in Dublin at this time, Alderman Henry Watson, a former mayor of

Limerick, raised concerns about reports in the New York newspapers of emigrants returning to Ireland to propagate republicanism. 'Such visitors combined with the rebellious clubs now forming, may be of some trouble to the state,' he observed. The Irish in America had indeed been electrified by the news of the revolutions in Europe, financial contributions making their way across the Atlantic, including £60 from the Robert Emmet Club of Cincinnati. So concerned were the British authorities, they actually arrested a number of American citizens upon their arrival in Ireland. James Bergen and Richard Ryan, prominent members of the IRU and putative leaders of the 'Irish brigade', were taken into custody in August and held for several months without charge, leading to a prolonged diplomatic dispute with the American government.[25]

A 'PACK OF ROBBERS'

On the night of Thursday 13 July, a jaded Thomas Francis Meagher arrived in Limerick city for the first time since the infamous riot. He had travelled down on the just completed Dublin to Limerick railway line and was met at the station 'by his confederates & a large number of the lower order'. A crowd gathered outside Cruise's Hotel and would not leave until Meagher got up from his bed to address them, delivering from his window 'a long speech, well seasoned with sedition, & concluded with offensive expressions toward the Lord

Portrait of William Smith O'Brien. *Courtesy of the Limerick City Museum*

Postcard showing Cahirmoyle House, Ardagh, Newcastle West,
County Limerick. *Courtesy of the Limerick City Museum*

Above: Location of the Sarsfield Club's rooms, 51 William Street, Limerick. *Author's Collection*

Left: Steel pike head made by Thomas Ahern, Vulcan Iron Works, 13 Catherine Street, Limerick. *Courtesy of the Limerick City Museum*

FRIDAY, APRIL 28, 1848.

Soiree to the Prosecuted Patriots.

ON SATURDAY Evening next, the 29th instant.
at Seven o'Clock. a Soiree will be given to

WILLIAM SMITH O'BRIEN ESQ. M·P··
JOHN MITCHELL,
AND
Thomas Francis Meagher, Esqrs..

to express the determination of the Repealers of this
City to sustain these
UNCOMPROMISING PATRIOTS
against the efforts of the British Government to crush
in their persons the liberties of the Irish Nation.

Tickets of Admission to the Soiree .. 2s 0d
SPECTATORS TO THE BOXES :
Ladies.. 1s 0d
Gentlemen...................................... 2s 0d

Tickets to be had at the REPOTRER OFFICE: the
EXAMINER OFFICE, at the Sarsfield Club Rooms, and
from the Secretary.

The Committee have limited the number of Tickets
and have taken measures to afford sufficient accommodation to all to whom tickets are issued.

(By order of the Committee,)
JOHN O'DONNELL, Secretary.
Limerick, April 25, 1848.

Advertisement in the *Limerick Reporter*, 28 April 1848.

Punch cartoon, 'The Battle of Limerick', 1848.
Courtesy of the Limerick City Museum

Left: Richard O'Gorman in America, 1860s. *Library of Congress, Washington, Prints & Photographs Division, LC–BH82-4608*

Below: The graves of John O'Donnell and Daniel Doyle, Mount St Lawrence Cemetery, Limerick. *Author's Collection*

Lieutenant'. The next day found Meagher in unusual company, dining at the George Street residence of the magistrate Dr William Geary. Geary was a former member of the Repeal Association who also sat on the board of the Waterford & Limerick Railway Company with Meagher's father. Another large crowd came together and the young orator stepped out onto his host's balcony from where he called the British government 'a murdering Government' and 'a robbing Government'.[26]

The following afternoon, Alderman Watson complained disbelievingly to the authorities in Dublin of how 'from the balcony of a *City magistrate*', Meagher (he writes Mitchel but clearly means Meagher) 'delivered another exciting speech, & impressed on the people of Limerick the necessity of organisation' and called the government 'a pack of robbers'. Geary, not surprisingly, was soon called upon to account for this. He explained that he was a long-standing friend of Meagher's father and had felt obliged to invite the younger Meagher to his home, good manners taking precedence over political differences. After their dinner, Geary, a doctor, had been called out on business. It was only when he returned home that he discovered the large assemblage calling on Meagher. He had, he claimed, been helpless to stop Meagher answering the crowd, and said the whole proceeding had filled him 'with deep pain'.[27] Geary's penitence sufficed and his explanation of events was deemed satisfactory.

Meagher was in the more familiar surroundings of the

Sarsfield Club a day after his dinner with Geary, meeting delegates from each of the confederate clubs in the city, now numbering five. The delegates took turns to read out addresses to the popular Young Ireland leader. James McCarthy of the Hugh O'Neill Club was the first to the floor, quickly followed by John McClenahan, editor of the *Limerick Reporter* and a member of the newly formed John Mitchel Club. R.W. Healy delivered the address of the Brian Boru Club, whilst John O'Donnell gave that of the host club, the Sarsfield Club. The address of the Treaty Stone Club, based in the working-class Thomondgate area of the city, was read out by Patrick McNamara, who stated: 'We are humble men, hard-working men, whose sole wealth is in their strong hands and toil-hardened sinews – we are little used to polished speech and nicely rounded phrases – we must speak plainly what we feel strongly.'[28]

Writing around the time of this meeting, Henry Watson described the Limerick clubs as 'composed chiefly of artisans'. This would certainly have been true of the Treaty Stone Club, the self-professed 'humble men, hard-working men' of Thomondgate. Their involvement in the Irish Confederation accords well with the argument that the clubs 'gave many young men of working-class backgrounds their first taste of direct participation in political affairs'.[29] The Limerick clubs, however, were not taken over by more militant figures in the aftermath of Mitchel's transportation as happened elsewhere. Despite the influx and importance of working-class members, it was the solicitors of the Sarsfield Club who remained the clear leaders of Young Ireland in the city.

Meagher listened attentively to the series of speeches before addressing the confederates gathered around him. He then spoke from the windows of the Sarsfield Club to the multitudes lining William Street, mischievously lauding the police and hoping 'some might be found to fraternise'. Meagher left for Tipperary on the five-o'clock train, delivering the next day a bracing speech to a 'monster meeting' on the summit of Slievenamon. According to Michael Doheny, the other main speaker on Slievenamon, at least 50,000 men (including O'Donnell and McClenahan) 'clambered [up] that steep mountain side, under a scorching July sun'.[30] It was an impressive, intimidating gathering, a sight to give great hope to the rebels and strike fear into the authorities.

The weather changed dramatically all over Ireland two days after the meeting at Slievenamon, a heavy wind from the west and incessant rains severely damaging the crops throughout Munster and presaging another poor harvest and continued famine. Yet hope and hardship continued to co-exist. The same issue of the *Reporter* that told of the potatoes in Limerick being once more diseased also carried a rousing poem entitled 'Ireland's Caution', the first verse of which read:

> Prepare, ye Men of '48 – the golden hour draws near
> When glory yet shall wreath your brows, or deck the
> crimson bier

When Hope's bright star, with vestal gleam, shall smile
  upon your way
And fling its radiance on your souls in Battle's darkest
  fray.[31]

THE 'RISING SPIRIT OF THE PEOPLE'

The vast expansion of the confederate club structure during the summer of 1848 opened it up to infiltration by police spies. The confederates were aware of the scale of the problem, members of the Swift Club in Dublin, for example, accusing each other of treachery and betrayal, and voicing a desire to catch informers and throw them down stairs and break their backs. The widespread infiltration of the clubs ensured that plans for a rebellion after the harvest were well known to the authorities in Dublin Castle. In early July, however, the Castle spies began to report on new plans for an outbreak at the beginning of August, before the harvest. It was perhaps one of these myriad informers who made public an apparently secret circular sent to the clubs in Cork naming 8 August as the date fixed for insurrection.[32]

Whatever the truth of that circular, Lord Clarendon had become extremely concerned about the intentions and abilities of the clubs. In June he ordered the under-secretary of state for Ireland, Thomas Redington, to send a confidential communiqué to the inspector general of police asking for 'court evidence' against the clubs.[33] He then ordered the arrest and imprisonment of the influential editors Duffy, Williams, O'Doherty and Martin on the night of 8–9 July. Ten days later, in a clear sign of a continuation of the clampdown, he proclaimed Dublin, Cork, Waterford and Drogheda. All inhabitants had to give up their weapons.

Writing just hours before the series of arrests, Richard O'Gorman described how the conduct of the police in Dublin was 'every day becoming more arbitrary and tyrannical'. The *Felon* office had just been seized and copies on the street were 'torn by the police from the hands of the news vendors'. The police tactics were clear: to 'intimidate' and 'break down' the 'rising spirit of the people' or 'to lash them into riot and premature outbreak'. O'Gorman hoped the people had the 'patient courage' to hold on for a few weeks longer. He nevertheless warned that all confederates 'should prepare their mind for what they may expect'. Everything seemed suddenly more serious.[34]

This series of arrests and proclamations forced the hand of the putative rebel leaders, and on the night of Friday 21 July a fateful meeting was held at O'Gorman's house at 23 Merchant's Quay in Dublin. Smith O'Brien, Meagher, John Blake Dillon and P.J. Smyth were all present, and it was decided that they should leave Dublin at once and 'go to certain Districts in the south and west of Ireland, supposed to be ripe for revolt, and which were then specially allotted to us' to 'place ourselves at the disposition of the People, to lead them or follow them, as events might determine'. O'Gorman was given charge of Limerick and Clare, and left Dublin within hours of the meeting. Smith O'Brien, O'Gorman recalled, 'was to take Tipperary, and keep up a communication with me, and generally direct my movements, so that they should cooperate with his own'.[35]

Arriving in Limerick city on the morning of Saturday 22 July, O'Gorman held a series of interviews with people 'supposed to be influential, who evinced great ardour and resolution, held out encouraging hopes [and] made statements as to the eagerness of the people for immediate action'. That evening, he visited four of the five confederate clubs in the city: the Sarsfield Club, the Brian Boru Club, the John Mitchel Club – where he had 'a silk handkerchief and pair of gloves' picked from his pocket – and the Hugh O'Neill Club. O'Gorman did not address only those members inside the club, but also the 'large masses of the people that congregated outside, who received him with every demonstration of enthusiasm'. For a bullish *Limerick Reporter*, words could not express 'the burning enthusiasm with which he was received in every Club' as he described 'the deadly tyranny under which the nation groans' and 'pointed out the duties and kindled the hopes of the people'.[36]

O'Gorman's movements were followed carefully by Henry Watson, the loyal alderman, who forwarded to Dublin an account describing how the Young Irelander had 'dealt out the usual disloyal oratory, abusing the Government, & calling on all who loved Ireland to form the clubs'. To the *Reporter*,

O'Gorman was 'a man of genius, heroism, and unblemished reputation – a man whose high character the breath of suspicion has never tainted'. He spoke out in a heartfelt if not particularly novel manner against the 'woes and oppressions of seven centuries' and the 'agonies and inhuman degradations of the late famine', each speech concluding with an exhortation to the audience to join clubs and '*prepare* in every way that became men who were not resolved to forego their manhood, and lie down as trampled serfs and slaves forever, under a foreign government'.[37]

The following morning, O'Gorman left the city to agitate and recruit in nearby Killaloe, County Clare. Several Limerick confederates, including O'Donnell and Doyle, accompanied him, as did a number of policemen taking notes. From Killaloe the group made their way across to Newport, County Tipperary, where a platform had been erected and where O'Gorman was 'introduced to the peasantry' by Bartholomew Dowling. Returning to Limerick city that evening – via a brief stop in Ahane – O'Gorman crossed the Shannon to the Treaty Stone Club in Thomondgate, addressing, according to the loyalist *Limerick Chronicle*, 'a formidable crowd in a strain of invective against tyranny and oppression'.

The success of O'Gorman's excursions was hotly contested in the Limerick journals: the *Limerick and Clare Examiner* claimed that ninety people enrolled immediately in a club in Killaloe, eighty more in one in Newport; in contrast, the *Chronicle* reported that in Killaloe the deputation had 'walked about for some time in despair, but ultimately they mustered a crowd of 300 idle persons, who were harangued in the usual inflammatory and seditious strain by Mr O'Gorman and the deputation', of whom no more than fifty enrolled in a club called the Kincora club. Henry Watson, likewise, provides a conflicting account of the mood and strength of the region's confederates. O'Gorman, he states correctly, met with 'no countenance from [Fr Vaughan] the P.P. of Killaloe'. Watson also believed 'several persons' had 'withdrawn from the Confederate Clubs in this City', and that 'a very extensive Club in Ennis was yesterday dissolved by its members'. Watson was forced to admit, however, that O'Gorman's 'mission' had 'done considerable mischief, particularly at Newport & in this City, by augmenting the Clubs to a very large extent'.[38]

Another aspect of Limerick's preparedness for revolt about which the newspapers disagreed was the bravery of the confederate club leaders. For the *Chronicle*, they were 'quite nervous, hourly dreading arrest', with several members resigning in terror. The *Reporter*, however, insisted that enthusiasm was undimmed, describing how, on the Sunday that O'Gorman was out agitating in Killaloe and Newport, the clubs in the city 'were visited by the Police, who asked for the names of the Presidents, Vice-Presidents, Secretaries, etc.' 'They got very little satisfaction, we believe, on any point,' proudly declared the *Reporter*, and 'were turned out of the Mitchel Club, where they obtruded themselves, one of the members stating to them that they could not be permitted to be present unless they became members, or had warrants'. Such visits, the *Reporter* averred, 'only increased the numbers and enthusiasm of the Clubs of this City'.[39]

THE 'REBELLIOUS MOVEMENT NOW ON FOOT'

Appropriating the idea from London on the day of the large Chartist rally, Samuel Maunsell, a magistrate in east Limerick, urged upon Lord Clarendon the use of 'special constables' in Ireland. For his own district of Cahirconlish, he suggested enrolling the loyal 'respectable tenant farmers' who had communicated their desire 'to be called upon to co-operate with the Authorities in the preservation of peace'. Maunsell was especially concerned by the return to Cahirconlish of a man named Ryan, 'who left this place for America about three months ago'. Ryan had returned 'from that country last evening *quite unexpectedly*, and from information which I have received I am led to suppose that his sudden return is in some way connected with the rebellious movement now on foot in this country'.[40]

The talks and wanderings of O'Gorman were a great worry for the gentry and magistrates of Limerick, and given the heavy strain on police resources, each area strongly pressed its own claims. The magistrates in Kilmallock wanted the police force recently sent to Kilfinane to be placed in their district instead. Their argument was that Kilmallock was located in 'the direct line between Dublin, Tipperary, Cork and Limerick' and would be 'the line taken in the event of any junction of the disaffected of these counties'. Their worries were exacerbated by the presence of a workhouse in the town and by the fact that the work on a nearby railway line gathered together in Kilmallock a large number of men, 'many of whom no doubt are disaffected, and who would be awed by the presence of a police force'. Edward Lloyd, a magistrate in the south of the county, wrote in dismay of the 'unprotected state' of his area, the majority of police having been dispatched to Newcastle West.[41]

Caleb Powell – the former MP for County Limerick, who lived a few miles outside of Castleconnell – had been quite friendly with Smith O'Brien in the 1830s. Their relationship, however, had deteriorated badly, culminating with Smith O'Brien's defeat of Powell at the 1847 general election. In late July 1848 Powell dispatched a letter to Thomas Redington complaining about police from his locality being 'withdrawn from it & assembled in Castleconnell'. Castleconnell was the home of some of the wealthiest citizens of Limerick and Powell acknowledged that there was little disaffection in the area, or clubs or other political organisations hostile to the government. Nevertheless, he felt 'the abandonment of the police station' was 'calculated not only to create alarm but considerable practical inconvenience in respect to the ordinary administration of justice'.[42] According to Powell, the 'pranks of Smith O'Brien and his confederates' were 'received not only with distrust, but disgust by all sorts & conditions of men in the eastern portion of the County Limerick'.[43]

Prosperous east Limerick – a part of the rich Golden Vale, the dairying heartland of Ireland – had a traditionally different mindset to the poorer, western part of the county, where support for the Young Irelanders was far stronger. In Abbeyfeale, for example, the shopkeeper Thomas Madigan was prosecuted for selling the *Irish Felon*. The Felon Club of Newcastle West, now numbering 220 members, went out on consecutive Sundays in July to the nearby villages to proselytise and organise clubs. The confederate club in Rathkeale – the Brian Boru Club – had up to 500 members. Furthermore, two police officers who had given evidence against Meagher were constantly hounded on the streets of Rathkeale, and even found pikes stuck into effigies of their bodies.[44] West Limerick, permanently shrouded in the smell of burning turf, proved a natural refuge for O'Gorman when the city became too dangerous for him.

6

INSURRECTION
AT ABBEYFEALE

Standing close to the border of Limerick and Cork, Bruree House, the country residence of Robert Fetherstone, was one of 'several handsome houses' in the barony of Upper Connello. Fetherstone, a local magistrate, was perturbed by the actions of the Young Irelanders, dispatching on Monday 31 July 1848 an anxious letter to his superiors in Dublin. Richard O'Gorman, he wrote, had passed through the area a few days earlier, agitating among the peasantry in advance of 'a simultaneous rising'. His call to arms had put the audience of landless labourers 'in a great state of excitement'. The wealthier farmers, however, were 'panic struck' and would 'take no part whatever' in the Young Irelander's rebellious designs.

Patently aware of the lack of real military experience in the Young Ireland ranks, O'Gorman, while in the vicinity of Bruree, had also made contact with a man named John Lynch, from Granagh, 'who had been an officer in the Spanish service'. Lynch, he hoped, would 'drill and take the command' of the local peasantry. Fetherstone, upon discovering these plans, sent immediately for Lynch, whom he believed 'to be a loyal and well affected gentleman'. His judgement proved unerringly correct, as Lynch told him he had declined 'to assume the command' even though he was warned 'he *should do* so or *mark* the consequences when called on'. Lynch also promised to communicate with Fetherstone 'should anything material occur'. Fetherstone concluded his letter with a generous offer that made clear the full extent of his unease. There were, he understood, fifty police 'to be stationed here today'. He proposed that 'should more accommodation be required a part of my House shall be at the disposal of the government'.[1] Like so many other members of the gentry then communicating with Dublin Castle, he wanted all the protection that was possible for his area. Fetherstone, however, need not have worried about accommodating any extra police, for, by the time of his writing, the Young Ireland rebellion, in the guise of an affray near the village of Ballingarry in County Tipperary, had been and gone.

'IN THE MIDST OF THE FIRE WITHOUT ANY PURPOSE'

The Young Ireland rebellion occurred on the afternoon of Saturday 29 July 1848. That morning, upon learning of the approach of a body of police from nearby Ballingarry, William Smith O'Brien and his band of a few hundred followers – peasants and colliers mostly – had barricaded the small village of the Commons. The troop of police, almost fifty strong and headed by Sub-Inspector Thomas Trant, escaped up a side road when a shot was fired at them from the barricades. A bellowing crowd from the Commons – about eighty strong and including many women – gave chase. The police took shelter in a large stone farmhouse a mile up the road and began to fire out the windows. Smith O'Brien and his followers – having been joined by Terence Bellew MacManus, a prominent confederate from Liverpool, and the twenty-four-year-old James Stephens, the future Fenian chief – took shelter behind the surrounding garden wall and outbuildings, their pikes and scythes waving in the air. They had, at most, twenty-two guns and pistols, and little ammunition.[2]

The exact sequence of events remains confused, clouded as it is by myriad partial and conflicting accounts. It appears, however, that Smith O'Brien and MacManus were discussing whether they should smoke out the police when the owner of the occupied farmhouse, a widow, Mrs McCormack, returned home. Sub-Inspector Trant was holding five of her young children hostage inside. Smith O'Brien entered the front garden to parley with the police. He sought their surrender and their arms, but to no avail. The police, in response to a volley of stones, then started firing again. Widow McCormack fled to her father's nearby house, and, over the course of the next hour, the affray spluttered on. The police, well armed and covered, were clearly in the ascendancy. The rebels, whose pikes and pitchforks were useless from a distance, suffered a number of casualties, including two dead: a stone-breaker called Thomas Walsh and a servant boy named Patrick McBride – a mere onlooker, a bewildered spectator at this strange event in rural Tipperary.

In MacManus' account of the rebellion, Smith O'Brien appears both resolute and lost, standing 'in the midst of the fire without any purpose'. MacManus urged a withdrawal back to the Commons, Smith O'Brien refused to countenance it. In the end, however, the peasant rebels – outnumbering the police but also hopelessly outgunned – began to abandon the field in their scores before scattering and disappearing into the mountains. With the approach of police reinforcements, MacManus combined with Stephens to finally drag their leader away. They put their 'rifles across his breast and drove him before us'.[3]

Smith O'Brien became separated from MacManus and Stephens in the aftermath of Ballingarry, and took refuge in the peasant houses of Tipperary. The Limerick newspapers speculated that he might be in the vicinity of Keeper Hill.[4] If so, Smith O'Brien was traversing the same stretch of land as the illustrious Patrick Sarsfield when, in an action subsequently known as 'Sarsfield's Ride', he destroyed a convoy of Williamite artillery at the time of the siege of Limerick in 1690. A number of other Young Ireland rebels, including Meagher, did indeed hide out on Keeper Hill, eluding, for a time, the police and troops scouring the countryside in search of them.

The *Cork Examiner* was among the first newspapers to carry definite-seeming news of the rebellion. A 'special reporter' was immediately dispatched to Tipperary to get the facts. His articles portrayed the stately Smith O'Brien as almost a wild vigilante, 'three loaded pistols in each of his waist belts', firing 'repeatedly at the police through the windows', and only retiring 'when his ammunition failed'. An old woman from Ballingarry swore she heard him say 'he would blow out his brains with one of his own pistols' if arrested.[5]

A week after the fateful engagement at Ballingarry, on the evening of Saturday 5 August, Smith O'Brien was arrested at Thurles railway station in County Tipperary. He had just purchased a second-class ticket for Limerick, and planned, if possible, to return home to Cahirmoyle. He made little effort to disguise himself; while walking through town earlier in the day, a few policemen had apparently whispered: 'For God's sake, Sir, why do you expose yourself so?' Smith O'Brien, however, was typically obstinate. He had on a number of occasions in the week leading up to Ballingarry stated to companions that he refused to be 'a fugitive where my fore-fathers reigned'.[6] This sentiment, it appears, guided him still; the heavy weight of his name was his passport and his burden, his making and, ultimately, his unmaking.

The 'special reporter' from the *Examiner* was also in Thurles at the time of the arrest, awaiting, rather fortuitously, the same train from Dublin. He was standing at the station a few minutes before eight o'clock when a man entered wearing 'a black hat, a blue boat coat in which he was rather tightly muffled, and a light plaid-like trousers'. The reporter immediately recognised Smith O'Brien, as did the railway guard, who informed some plainclothes detectives. Smith O'Brien was swiftly apprehended by the detectives, who shoved him 'in the roughest manner possible'. The weary Young Ireland leader did not resist his arrest even though he carried a pistol and a large black stick. His only words were 'easy – take me easy', which he repeated 'with the greatest mildness of tone, and apparent suavity of temper'.[7] He was taken to the local police station for a couple of hours before being conveyed that night on a special train to Kilmainham Gaol in Dublin.

The *Examiner* broke the news of Smith O'Brien's arrest in a special edition on Sunday 6 August, issued in place of its regular Monday edition. A few days later, it carried a report, taken from the *Manchester Guardian*, on the railway guard, William Hulme, who had pointed out Smith O'Brien to the detectives. Hulme had been a policeman in Manchester for a number of years before leaving to work as a porter at Victoria railway station in London. He then moved across to Ireland to join the Great Southern & Western Railway. He had an audience with Lord Clarendon in the week following the arrest and received a reward of £500 for his part in Smith O'Brien's capture.[8] The ceremony, quite maliciously, was held at the Bank of Ireland buildings on College Green, the site of the old Irish parliament that Smith O'Brien longed to restore.

AN 'UNWILLING COCKPIT OF REBELLION'

The week leading up to Ballingarry had been filled for the Young Irelanders with frantic activity and alternating moods of hope and despair. On the morning of Saturday 22 July 1848, news reached Dublin that a bill to suspend habeas corpus was being rushed through parliament in London, a dramatic action that allowed anyone suspected of treason to be imprisoned without trial. That night, Meagher and Dillon, having evaded the eyes of the police, travelled down on the mail coach to Wexford. They found Smith O'Brien at about six o'clock on Sunday morning, asleep in the house of an old friend, John Maher, and told him of the turn of events. The three confederates began to discuss where best to stage their now inevitable rebellion, finally fixing on the city of Kilkenny.

The reasons for selecting Kilkenny were manifold. Its inland location, according to Meagher, made it impervious to all 'war-steamers, gunboats, floating batteries', its streets were 'extremely narrow' and ideal for the 'erection of barricades', the army barracks was outside the city, and the main roads leading in were lined by steep embankments from which the rebels could fire on and 'cut to pieces' whole regiments. Furthermore, the bridge over the River Nore could be 'demolished' very easily and an imminent agricultural show meant the bellies of insurgents would be filled with 'the choicest beef and mutton'. Kilkenny, bordered by 'the three best fighting counties in

Ireland – Waterford, Wexford and Tipperary', was also among the areas least affected by the Famine.

The hope, for Meagher, was that a successful outbreak 'in a thinly garrisoned district' would prove the spark for a national insurrection. All that was required was a strong martial spirit to see the plan through. This, however, was precisely the ingredient Kilkenny lacked. The three rebels arrived on Sunday evening and were immediately informed by the leading confederate, Robert Cane, that the clubs in the city 'were insufficiently armed, miserably so indeed', and that there was no possibility of starting the rising there.[9] The cold rebuff was greatly disheartening considering the emphasis the leaders placed on a decisive, inspiring opening action.

With Kilkenny proving an unwilling cockpit of rebellion, Smith O'Brien, Meagher and Dillon took a carriage the next morning to Carrick-on-Suir, a large town straddling the three counties of Tipperary, Waterford and Kilkenny. Carrick appeared to be well organised, with at least eleven clubs, more than 1,000 confederates and even a central committee for coordination. Its strength, however, was more on paper than in reality, the membership figures inflated by a sizeable number of Old Irelanders who had joined 'United Repealers' clubs but who had no interest in physical force. Michael Doheny, riding into Carrick on horseback, a day after Smith O'Brien's arrival, had 'envied the destiny which God had awarded to its inhabitants, in breaking the first link of the slavery of nearly twenty generations'. He did not remain so hopeful for long. Rebellious fervour was sorely absent, and the three Young Irelanders had hardly entered the town before they were beset with questions along the lines of 'why should Carrick be selected?'[10]

Carrick wavered when called to rebellion, and the three leaders left that evening for Cashel in County Tipperary, the home of Doheny. Here, on Tuesday 25 July, they met again that mix of consternation and fear that showed the true hollowness of the clubs' earlier words of strong action. Doheny had unfortunately gone off to find Smith O'Brien in Carrick, and his absence from Cashel 'was used as an argument, sincere or pretended, against any effort in that town'.[11] The majority of Young Ireland clubmen simply were not prepared to launch or engage in a full insurrection.

One after the other, Kilkenny, Carrick and Cashel stalled or pleaded helplessness. The rebel leaders were cheered on the streets but found no succour in private discussions with club leaders, the chasm between their words and actions insurmountable. This scenario would most likely have been repeated no matter what three towns or cities the rebels called on, with the exception, perhaps, of Dublin. The capital, however, had early on been discounted as a centre of rebellion because of the overwhelming military presence. Among the myriad excuses rolled out by the clubmen of Kilkenny, Carrick and Cashel was a grave lack of arms. Both the Young Ireland leaders and the clubmen themselves were to blame for this want of martial preparedness. The leaders had been far from diligent in ensuring the country was properly stockpiled with weapons, a basic necessity of any uprising. In 1798, for example, while other material was light, pikes at least were in profusion. The clubmen, for their part, were guilty of months of self-serving bluster that led one spy in Dublin to report on the supposed availability of up to 20,000 old flint guns, to be sold at eight shillings and sixpence each.[12]

Meagher separated from Smith O'Brien after Cashel, returning to Waterford to try and raise men there. Smith O'Brien and Dillon, joined now by Patrick O'Donohoe and James Stephens – a bullish young confederate from Kilkenny quickly appointed by Smith O'Brien as his aide-de-camp – got two jaunting cars ready and took to the hills. O'Donohoe, a relatively minor Dublin clubman, had travelled down to Kilkenny on the prompting of Charles Gavan Duffy, still imprisoned in Newgate. In Kilkenny, he had initially been mistaken for a spy; one of the two men, in fact, who falsely accused and then detained O'Donohoe was Stephens. O'Donohoe, however, was a well-treated captive; as the three men (O'Donohoe, Stephens and another Young Irelander named Kavanagh) travelled through the rainy night to Thurles and then Cashel, they sipped generously on poitín along the way.[13] Once suspicions of O'Donohoe's loyalty had been allayed, this revolutionary cabal – first gaining and then losing hundreds of recruits – spent the next few days in constant motion between the three rugged mountainside villages of Killenaule, Mullinahone and Ballingarry.

Monaghan-born Terence Bellew MacManus caught up

with the rebels in Ballingarry on the morning of Thursday 27 July. In his mid-thirties, MacManus was one of the leading confederates in England. He worked as a shipping agent in Liverpool and had actually been followed over to Ireland by a detective. His pursuer, however, lost sight of him in Dublin. MacManus had earlier been involved in organising fund-raisers for the poor Irish pouring into Liverpool and was also engaged in some business with the Cork-based Young Irelander and distiller, Denny Lane. Although his business was struggling, MacManus still arrived in Tipperary with enough money to buy bread and supplies for scores of men.[14] He was, therefore, an exception to the rule in a country so ravaged by famine, a factor Smith O'Brien seemed not to take into account when he gave his infamous, idiosyncratic order that there was to be no plunder of food from surrounding estates. The standards of moral probity Smith O'Brien set for himself – even in time of insurrection – were not just exacting but simply impossible for men of lesser means to attain or even comprehend.

The last days before rebellion saw Smith O'Brien, pistols in hand, drill hundreds and sometimes thousands of men till late at night in Mullinahone and Ballingarry. His mood, however, veered between buoyant and tearful. There were celebrations when he entered villages, but also arguments with more radical Young Irelanders. In addition, the constant marching, the lack of sleep and heavy rains were draining. The near-complete lack of sympathy from his family was a further source of distress; a note from his sister-in-law Ellen to her brother, the poet Aubrey de Vere, condemned Smith O'Brien's 'infamous conduct', and described how his 'poor mother is very unhappy & so is poor little Lucy'. About Smith O'Brien's pregnant wife Lucy, she added: 'The clouds seem to gather round her daily more hopelessly & she looks upon a long & dreary separation as almost inevitable.'[15]

The men who marched with Smith O'Brien were predominantly poorly fed, ill-clothed and miserably armed peasants from the surrounding countryside. There were also a number of colliers from the local coalfields. Followers, it seems, were to be had, but could not be kept, the rebel army haemorrhaging numbers and dwindling from 4,000 to a few hundred in a matter of days. Some evaporated on account of the aimlessness of Smith O'Brien and the other leaders. The majority, though, left because of the priests who went amongst them and instructed them to return home. Words of heaven and hell, of God and the devil, made a deep impression on the peasants' minds. The rebel priests, meanwhile – among them Fr John Kenyon of Templederry and Fr James Birmingham of Borrisokane – had been cowed by their bishop, and went quiet for the last vital weeks of July.

A notion of gathering men in preparation for a march on Kilkenny guided the rebels' movements, but nothing was certain. Then even this vague plan was lost as Smith O'Brien determined to stay on in the mountains until after the harvest, just a fortnight away. He informed the other leaders of this decision on the evening of Friday 28 July when they convened in Thomas Sullivan's pub in the small colliery village of the Commons. The leaders – not all of whom were convinced by Smith O'Brien's tactics – split up soon afterwards to agitate in various parts of the country. Meagher, who had only just rejoined Smith O'Brien having failed to muster men in Waterford, was sent back there with O'Donohoe and two others. Doheny returned to Slievenamon, while Dillon went west to his home territory of Roscommon and Mayo. Smith O'Brien asked MacManus and Stephens to remain with him in the area around Ballingarry. The next day came the rising, when Smith O'Brien and the Young Ireland rebels finally lost control over events – that is, if they had ever actually been in control.

HUE AND CRY

News of the suspension of habeas corpus reached Limerick the Monday before the rebellion, just as Smith O'Brien was endeavouring to raise Carrick. Learning also 'that a large reward was offered for my arrest', Richard O'Gorman decided 'on consultation' that he 'should leave the City of Limerick, and extend the Club organisation through the County'. Two members of the Sarsfield Club, John O'Donnell and Daniel Doyle, travelled with him, and proved steadfast companions during the tumultuous weeks that followed. They proceeded first to Rathkeale, 'where a large meeting was held, and from that time, we continued to hold public meetings in the towns and large villages, concealing ourselves at night as best we could, so as to avoid arrest'.[16]

The description of O'Gorman in *Hue and Cry*, the police bulletin, read:

> Richard O'Gorman, jun., barrister; thirty years of age; five feet eleven inches in height; very dark hair; dark eyes; thin long dark face; large dark whiskers; well made and active, walks upright, dress black frock coat, tweed trousers.

Hue and Cry was often factually incorrect; O'Gorman was closer to twenty-seven than thirty. His profile, however, was quite accurate and far less demeaning than Smith O'Brien's, who was said to have 'a sneering smile constantly on his face'. In similar vein, John Blake Dillon supposedly had a 'bilious look' and Michael Doheny the 'coarse red face' of 'a man given to drink'.[17]

O'Gorman left west Limerick in the middle of the week, travelling through the south of the county towards Tipperary in search of his leader: 'Day after day, I expected intelligence of Smith O'Brien, but received none – I sent messengers to him, who never returned to me – some, as I was afterwards informed, were arrested on the way.' Concerned by this lack of contact, O'Gorman 'went into the town of Tipperary and from thence sent on one of … [his] companions in search of O'Brien. He failed to find him, but learned from one of his people that he was at Ballingarry.' This was probably on the morning of Thursday 27 July. 'From that place, O'Brien sent me a message, directing me to return to the County Limerick – to continue the organisation I had begun there and to await further orders from him.' O'Gorman told how he 'heard nothing more of O'Brien, until news reached me of his arrest'.[18]

THE 'PATRIOT SONS OF IRELAND'

The final week of July found the country absorbed in eager talk of the Young Irelanders. News travelled slowly in Ireland in 1848, however, and so rumours and whispers filled the newspapers. Had Carrick risen, or Kilkenny? Did Michael Doheny have an army ready on Slievenamon? In Limerick, 'the thoughts of everyone' were 'engrossed with concern for the patriot sons of Ireland'. Groups huddled 'in various quarters of the city, engaged in conversation, and discussing the consequences of the Government's last act': the suspension of habeas corpus. Crowds greeted 'the arrival of each train' in search of news, but the accounts were all 'various and con-flicting'. Meanwhile, notices about the rewards on offer for the capture of Smith O'Brien and his comrades 'were scarcely posted up in the various parts of the city … when they were either torn down or defaced'.[19]

For the *Limerick Reporter*, 'fixed purpose' and 'stern resolve' filled every mind in the city. This assertion quickly proved false, as O'Gorman found on his return to Limerick, where he 'received definite and reliable information from the City … which convinced me that all hope of cooperation there was gone, and that the movement had so far been a failure'. A fresh proclamation from Lord Clarendon banning the clubs had unnerved the confederates of Limerick city, as it had many others around the country. As with Kilkenny, Carrick and Cashel, their rebellious strength proved illusory, dissipating swiftly when faced with the heavy weight of the law. West Limerick, wild and remote, remained a different proposition, and it was to here that O'Gorman and his cohorts now returned, with reports appearing of the police 'in active pursuit of Mr O'Gorman' near Cahirmoyle.[20]

O'Gorman and his companions, O'Donnell and Doyle, made it safely to Abbeyfeale near the border of Limerick and Kerry. On the evening of Thursday 3 August they addressed a large crowd a mile outside the town before heading on to Athea. O'Gorman at this stage was still unaware of the defeat at Ballingarry. He urged the people of Abbeyfeale to arm themselves and to form a rebel camp similar to that which existed during the time of the Rockite uprising of 1821–24.[21] A zealous plainclothes detective learned of the meeting and set off to arrest the Young Irelanders. He was recognised before he could get there, however, and was 'taken prisoner by the Mob'. According to Michael Galway, the local magistrate, the detective was relieved of 'his Pistols, Money, and everything he had'. John Fitzgerald, the postmaster at Abbeyfeale, related how the '*detective was Detected* and it is a miracle that he did not lose his life', paraded as he was 'thro' the street here amongst the booing & every other insult of men women & children'. The captured detective had 'a Guard of Twelve Armed Men', who intended to hand him over to O'Gorman. A few of their number caught up with O'Gorman on his way to Athea, but he instructed them to let the prisoner go. The detective, bloodied and bruised, was 'liberated' at ten o'clock that night, and had his money and clothes returned to the magistrate. His pistols were kept, though, and that night 'no person in town' would provide him with accommodation. He was eventually 'taken to a cabin out of town where he lay until morning'. This was the beginning rather than the end of disturbances in the district, with Sub-Inspector Coppinger being shot at in the street the following night. Then a shop-keeper – a former police sergeant suspected of being in league with the detective – had his life threatened and his business boycotted.[22]

'ARMED MEN ON THE HILLS'

In response to the attack on the detective and the reported stealing of arms 'from several persons' nearby, Michael Galway, the magistrate at Abbeyfeale, drafted extra police in from Newcastle West. The postmaster John Fitzgerald felt this move only 'added to the excitement' in the area, and on the morning of Saturday 5 August 1848, the west Limerick rebels attacked the mail coaches travelling between Limerick and

Tralee, Abbeyfeale being the halfway point. For Fitzgerald, the 'Rising here' stemmed directly from the activities of the '*Detective* who came in coloured clothes to arrest or trail out Mr O'Gorman'. Had 'he come in his proper uniform', people said, he would not have been so 'molested', plainclothes detectives being particularly loathed and distrusted figures of authority at this time.[23]

The road through Abbeyfeale – linking Limerick, Tralee and Caherciveen – was a major artery in Ireland's growing road network. As a main route for coaches, it had a metalled surface (that is, made with broken stones) about 18 feet wide, with gravel borders. The 'insurrection', as it was called, took place 'an English mile' on the Kerry side of the town, a short distance from Feale Bridge. The two coaches were 'within about six perches of each other' when 150 rebels raced out from behind a thick covering of whitethorn bushes to seize the horses and halt the drivers. A large number were armed with double-barrelled shotguns, while others carried pikes and pitchforks. Daniel Harnett – who called himself a captain under 'General O'Gorman' – and Michael Denniston were among the leaders of the attack. They were, in the main, 'well-dressed men', wearing tweed coats cut 'in the shooting jacket fashion'.[24]

The first coach to be stopped was that travelling up from Tralee to Limerick. The guard on this coach, Galvin, said that as well as those involved in the hold-up, 'he saw about 500 more armed men on the hills and taking shelter under the rocks in the neighbourhood', though this might have been an exaggeration to save face. The rebels, he continued, 'threatened to saw up the Coach … if the mails and arms were not given up quietly'. Galvin heeded the threats and had two blunderbusses taken from him. The rebels then got the mailbags but no guns from the second coach, as the guard, Purcell, had 'concealed them having had some intimation at Abbeyfeale of the probability of an attack'. Having sent the coaches on their way, the insurgents, 'sounding horns, leisurely walked off the road through the mountains, in the direction of the village of Brosna' in County Kerry. It was supposed that O'Gorman was 'in the part of the mountains to which the insurgents directed their steps'.[25]

Fitzgerald, the postmaster, was approached within a few hours of the raid by a person 'saying that one of the leaders' wanted to see him 'in order to give me back the bags'. He consulted with Galway and Coppinger. They wanted to send a police escort with Fitzgerald, but he preferred to go alone, 'in dread I would lose my life'. He met four of the leaders that night, 'who began opening the bags and also all official letters and letters to & for policemen. Some of the official ones they kept & returned some more after reading them.' The rebels 'also met one letter which was registered and asked what was the green cover for. I said it may be it contained money. They said they did not mean to deprive any man of his property', and wanted only to obstruct government communications. The mailbags were then returned, albeit jumbled up, and Fitzgerald got a farmhand from nearby – who had a horse and cart – to help carry them back to Abbeyfeale.[26]

The attack on the mail coaches made front-page news as far away as New York, where an amplified account had Galvin 'knocked off' his seat 'by the stroke of a gun' and threatened with his life. It was a cause of concern, too, for Ireland's business community. Charles Bianconi, for example – the coaching magnate who operated out of Clonmel in County Tipperary – worried that any disruption of the mails would spread to the passenger services he ran on the same roads. Bianconi made contact with Thomas Redington, the under-secretary, enclosing a copy of a speech he had made in 1843 that highlighted the benefits his business brought to local communities, not least the purchases of hay and oats. Bianconi underlined for emphasis a sentence that said how the business had 'never met any interruption in the performance of its arduous duties'. Bianconi would have been pleased with the quick response of the authorities, who gave police protection to the mails travelling between Tralee and Limerick. The postmaster general suspended Galvin and Purcell, the un-fortunate coach guards, for not offering enough resistance. They had each more than twenty years' service.[27]

The attack on the mail coaches seemed at first a mere prelude to even deadlier actions, with Michael Galway, the magistrate, describing to Redington how 'the Insurgents' had 'formed an encampment in the County of Kerry within one Mile of the Town' and were 'in possession of a great deal of Fire

Arms'. It was rumoured, he continued, that 'they will come in to Town tomorrow'. John Fitzgerald corroborated these fears. 'The country is in a dreadful state', he insisted, and 'it is God only knows what will happen on tomorrow (Sunday) as the Rebels told me it was their firm intention to enter this town with a view of attacking the police'. Duffy portrayed the rebels eagerly debating 'whether they would unite to form a junction with the force which they expected O'Gorman to lead, or attack the town at once'. The grand assault never materialised, however, the 'evil news from Tipperary' filtering through to west Limerick at last, dismaying the rebels and putting them to flight in the hills.[28]

O'Gorman, looking back on his time in west Limerick, took some satisfaction at least in the fact that 'with many men half armed, undisciplined and reckless' about him day and night, 'there was no case of any outrage committed by any of them on life, limb, or property – no disgrace of that kind was attached to the movement'. The end did not justify the means for O'Gorman any more than for Smith O'Brien, the 'genteel rebel' who 'promised only glory – not confiscated estates'.[29] They would prefer a failed rebellion to one morally flawed.

7

'ON THE RUN'

In the dark of night on Saturday 12 August 1848, Thomas Francis Meagher, Patrick O'Donohoe and Maurice Leyne – another Young Irelander – were arrested in County Tipperary. Travelling east along the road linking Clonoulty with Holycross, and unsure of their bearings, the three fugitives encountered by grave mischance a body of patrolling policemen. This was a week after the arrest of William Smith O'Brien, a week in which Meagher and his companions had scarcely left the environs of Slievenamon. For several days, a local parish priest, Fr Mackey of Carrigeen, had provided them with shelter; his curate, Fr Carroll, described the three 'forlorn figures' as 'somewhat dishevelled from constant walking', with shoes 'quite broken' and 'soiled by many days wear', and coats and trousers 'clotted with mud and heavy with damp'.[1]

The prisoners were taken to Kilmainham Gaol in Dublin, where they were reunited with the incarcerated Smith O'Brien. They were joined a few weeks later by Terence Bellew MacManus, who was arrested on board a vessel in Cork

Harbour, having come agonisingly close to escape. Smith O'Brien's pregnant wife Lucy took lodgings near Kilmainham and visited him regularly, as did the whole family, who now rallied around him. He also spent a portion of each day giving lessons to his eldest son Edward. The other prisoners amused themselves with less cerebral pursuits, such as signing their autographs in the books and cards sent into them for mementos and playing marbles in the yard. Meagher, ever the gentleman, sent the gift of a book to Anne Mackey, the sister and house-keeper of the priest who had aided him. O'Donohoe was least at ease and needed to 'drink grog to keep up his spirits'.[2]

Prison life was less comfortable for the scores of impove-rished peasants and colliers implicated in Smith O'Brien's uprising and picked up during the great sweep of arrests that followed Ballingarry, police and troops having flooded the most disturbed districts in the country. Tipperary had been a natural focus for the authorities. West Limerick was another, with O'Gorman supposedly having formed a rebel camp there, and having staged an attack on a commissariat store.[3]

'DOGGED, WORRIED AND HUNTED DOWN'

On Wednesday 9 August 1848, the conservative *Limerick Chronicle* reported with satisfaction that there 'was no excitement whatever in this City on receipt of the intelligence of Mr Smith O'Brien's arrest'. Limerick city had been cowed by the show of strength by the lord lieutenant and British authorities. West

Limerick was a different story: two companies of the 88th Regiment, stationed in Tralee, were dispatched to guard bridges around Abbeyfeale and Newcastle West 'which the people expressed themselves determined to destroy'. These soldiers, along with an additional 200 police drafted into the area, met an extremely cold reception in Abbeyfeale. The locals adopted a system of passive resistance and refused to sell them any goods or provisions – not even 'a grain of tea or sugar' was traded, one witness observed. Eventually, Sub-Inspector Coppinger ordered the police to just take what supplies they needed and to leave the appropriate money on the counter.[4]

The augmented police force set to work on rounding up those involved in the troubles. Michael Galway, the relatively new magistrate for the area, was said to be 'out every night and … indefatigable in his exertions to find out and take the parties who robbed the mails'. For the *Chronicle*, 'all the fellows' involved in the incident were known to the police and likely to be caught very quickly, even allowing for the vast tracts of mountain range they had for hiding. Such confidence seemed well placed when eighteen men were arrested just days later. Scores more arrests followed – including that of Michael Denniston, one of the leaders of the attack – placing a heavy burden on the already overcrowded county jails.[5]

Patrick McCormack, just returned to the country after eleven years in America, was among those taken in for questioning. His claim to have been holidaying in Killarney was met with suspicion. Galway – 'struck by his foreign appearance' and wary as all the authorities were of an influx of Irish-American insurgents – thought McCormack had been in contact with O'Gorman and ordered his bags to be opened; the search yielded nothing more incriminating than two 'soiled shirts'. McCormack, nevertheless, was accompanied to Limerick city by an officer and brought before Pierce George Barron. McCormack's account of his activities 'not being satisfactory', the Limerick magistrate ordered another police escort for McCormack up to Dublin, as he had a ticket for a ship sailing from there to America. The magistrate also suggested that McCormack's lodgings in Dublin should be 'marked'.[6]

Charles Newton, an Englishman travelling through Bruff, suffered a similarly discomfiting fate, being dragged out of a mail coach 'in the most unceremonious manner' by two policemen he described as ruffians. One of the officers went through Newton's 'private papers' and, he said, threatened 'to strike me with his baton'. Newton, an employee of a telegraph company in Sheffield, had been mistaken for O'Gorman. He was, however, a stout, thickset man of 'about middle size' with very light hair, and nothing at all like O'Gorman. He was detained for almost an hour and only released following the interjection of a fellow passenger, a magistrate from Tipperary named Croker.[7]

Known members of confederate clubs were obvious targets for the police. William Fuller Hartnett, president of the Felon Club in Newcastle West, was arrested for 'treasonable practices' in the middle of August. Later that month, Thomas

McNamara (solicitor), Richard O'Shaughnessy (grocer) and Michael O'Neill (stonemason) – all former members of the Brian Boru Club in Rathkeale – were marched to jail in Limerick city by a body of dragoons, while at Newcastle West fair, a man named Walsh was taken into custody for singing a ballad called 'Mitchel's Farewell to Ireland'.[8]

This spate of arrests clearly frightened John Norris, a classics' teacher and member of the Felon Club in Newcastle West. He wrote directly to Lord Clarendon in a bid for clemency, insisting that during his 'short connection with the Club' he had only ever advocated moral force. He had, he said, left 'the Society for good and all on the 10th of July, and sent notice to Mr Coppinger the Sub-Inspector of Police, to that effect, on the 20th of said month'. He had since then been called a coward, and 'avoided and frowned at through the street'. He was, he informed the lord lieutenant, 'a man advanced in years, and encumbered with a wife and young children, and consequently an out and out enemy to Civil War'. He stressed that he 'never had any military or warlike weapon, and the opportunity of Newspapers was my chief motive for joining the Club', and even offered a local priest, Fr Cregan, as a reference. The letter, or more likely the earlier communication with Coppinger, seems to have worked, as Norris does not appear among the names of those arrested. He was, however, far more involved in the confederate organisation than he made out and had been instrumental in the establishment of smaller clubs around the district. He was also a writer, with a number of his poems having been published in the local newspapers, including a lament for Daniel O'Connell.[9]

The determination of Michael Galway to capture the outlaws and clear the proclaimed district of arms was undimmed. On 14 August he detailed how 'a large body of Police patrolled the country last night', travelling more than twenty miles and searching numerous houses for weapons. Two days later, he described Coppinger going out with a force of twenty men and returning with four prisoners, one of whom was identified as leading the attack on the detective. In October two more men involved in that attack, Thomas Denniston and Denis Twomey, were captured, having hidden in the mountains of Kerry for two months. Galway also got a local priest to 'address his flock from the Altar ... as to the surrendering of Arms'. The priestly invocation does not appear to have succeeded, as on the last day of August a man named Michael Herlihy was arrested for having a blunderbuss 'concealed in the thatch of an outhouse'.[10]

Galway's chief focus, besides O'Gorman, was the capture of the elusive Daniel 'Danny Dan' Harnett and Charles Hughes, two leading confederates in west Limerick. Harnett, a 'bold and resolute young fellow' according to Duffy, was the leader of the Abbeyfeale rebels. The *Limerick Reporter* celebrated his:

> ... hair-breadth escapes from the police – his agility in
> bounding over the crags and fastnesses of his mountain
> home – his reckless daring in passing frequently through
> the town in open day and under the eyes of the spies and

detectives, who watch his movements and thirst for his capture – his undisturbed security – his buoyancy and cheerfulness in all his perils, and his fortitude in bearing up against the fate intended for him – the fate of a political outlaw who always detested the misrule of the English Government in Ireland.

He was, the panegyric continued, 'always charitable and humane, cheerful and jocose, generous to a proverb, often dividing his own meal with the hungry beggar at his door'. It was no wonder, the newspaper concluded, that he was 'idolised by his neighbours and numerous friends, and harboured from arrest'.

Hughes, too, received generous praise from the *Reporter*. A simple nailer from Abbeyfeale, he had from boyhood been 'passionately fond of books' even earning the sobriquet 'The Novelist'. He had read fiction at first, 'and few novels escaped him'. In later years, however, he had turned his attention to books describing the 'history and antiquities' of Ireland. He had 'imbibed the Young Ireland spirit', and 'few of that body had such antipathy to English dominion in Ireland'. Accused of being a principal in the attack on the mail coaches, the 'poor forlorn tradesman' was now 'dogged, worried, and hunted down as if he were the most powerful foe in the world to the British Government'.[11]

Galway came close to the capture of these two 'principals of the late Insurrectionary Movement' in early October, missing them by just ten minutes after being told by an informer where they were drinking. Hughes, indeed, had come into town looking for a book – to fill the empty hours up in the mountains, most likely. In November Galway reported on the arrest of two men, Patrick Roche and John Crowley, 'for obstructing and deceiving the Constabulary' when in pursuit of Hughes. 'I regret to say,' the magistrate continued, 'that such obstruction is very much the habit of the people here.'[12]

THE 'UNWANTED ATTENTIONS OF THE POLICE'

Limerick city was much quieter than the county in the aftermath of the failed Young Ireland rising. There were no rallies outside the rooms of the now proclaimed Sarsfield Club, or demonstrations on the streets. The clubmen laid low and were not subjected to the same scale of arrests seen in cities such as Cork. The presence of foreigners was looked on with suspicion, and two Swiss citizens were detained briefly at the beginning of August. Emigrant ships lying in port were combed for O'Gorman, John O'Donnell and Daniel Doyle. O'Donnell's house at 9 William Street was also searched one Sunday morning, yielding up 'several documents and private communications ... connected with the late movements'.[13]

John McCormack was one member of the Sarsfield Club to receive the unwanted attentions of the police: he was arrested in Kilkee, County Clare, for 'treasonable practices'. McCormack, who had been the owner of the Limerick Brush

Factory, was not held for long and soon emigrated to New South Wales in Australia, his factory having been burned down in early August.[14]

John McClenahan, the forthright editor of the *Limerick Reporter*, was another confederate to experience an unplanned encounter with the police. According to Thomas D'Arcy McGee, one of the Young Ireland leaders in Dublin, the *Reporter* seceded 'from the movement in the hour of danger', the proprietor James Rutherford Browne less enamoured of rebellion than McClenahan. This was, after all, a time when the owners and editors of journals the length and breadth of the country – including Marron of the *Drogheda Argus* and Butler of the *Galway Vindicator* – were being seized. McClenahan left the *Reporter* in early August and travelled to his wife's home town in west Kerry. He was arrested there on Tuesday 15 August 'on suspicion of being a political runaway', but was released when it was discovered there was no warrant out for his arrest. The young man who informed on McClenahan was then forced 'to fly for his life from Caherciveen', where the editor's wife's family were well respected.[15]

The *Limerick Chronicle* accused McClenahan of absconding from Limerick in fear. He replied indignantly, stating that he had not fled anywhere but was merely visiting relatives and had 'appeared in public openly and undisguised'. If he was worried about arrest, he asked, why would he have gone to County Kerry where he was so well known? 'The truth is,' he opined, 'I was mistaken for a far greater man – a man with a prize of £300 attached to his name.'[16] By this, he meant, of course, the elusive O'Gorman.

'HUNTED FROM PLACE TO PLACE'

On Monday 31 July 1848, the *Cork Examiner* published a letter under the heading 'Rumoured death of O'Gorman'. 'I suppose, 'ere this,' suggested the writer, 'you have heard of the fate of poor O'Gorman. Two gentlemen have just arrived from Tarbert, who state they have seen his remains at the Police Station-house.' The Limerick newspapers gave the story little credence; their scepticism proved quickly correct when it emerged that an Edward Gorham had just committed suicide near Tarbert. The similar-sounding names and apparent physical resemblance had caused the confusion.[17] This was not, however, the last erroneous account of O'Gorman to appear in the papers. In fact, it was just the first in a litany of often ludicrous stories.

Charles Gavan Duffy has described the newspapers of Ireland as 'filled for weeks with stories of O'Gorman's hair-breadth escapes and romantic adventures'. There were sightings of him all over Munster, from Dunmanway in west Cork to Miltown Malbay in Clare, and at his uncle's house in the centre of Waterford city. Spy reports placed him in custody in Dublin. In Kilrush, a large wooden container carrying a piano was opened and searched for him. In Birr in County Offaly, a man named O'Gorman was attacked on the street, his assailant calling out for the police, convinced that he had just won £300. The police simply laughed and the attacker slunk away amidst the jeers of the crowd.[18]

One story to attract a great deal of attention depicted O'Gorman avoiding capture in the disguise of a lady. He was even said to have taken the arm of a magistrate while disembarking from a steamer in Kilrush. This tale, first published in the Dublin Castle newspaper, the *Dublin Evening Post*, was robustly denied in the narrative of Michael Doheny. It has proved resilient, however, continuing to appear as fact in modern works on Young Ireland.[19]

By the end of August, reports were abroad that O'Gorman had 'landed in France' with 'two proscribed gentlemen of this city, who attended him in his wanderings and hair-breadth escapes during the last fortnight'. One French paper, *Le Constitutionnel*, described him arriving in a fishing boat off the coast of Brest. *The Sunday Times* had him already sojourning in Paris. A report in the *Pilot*, meanwhile, from an authority 'upon which we can hardly cast a shadow of doubt', placed O'Gorman and his cohorts three weeks out to sea, having escaped on board an America-bound vessel.[20] None of these stories was correct, and some may even have been planted to distract the attention of the police. Others were perhaps genuine but confused, mixing up O'Gorman with the scores of Irish felons who *did* manage to get to France – John O'Mahony and James Stephens, the two future leaders of the Fenian movement, most prominent among this number.

O'Gorman's movements during the hazardous months of August and September are difficult to trace as he did not leave a detailed account like Doheny's *The Felon's Track*. He did write a short narrative for Duffy (then preparing his *magnum opus* on Young Ireland) in the summer of 1881, but found his memory was 'scarcely reliable either as to incidents themselves, or as to the exact order of time in which they took place'.[21] It seems certain, however, that he stayed around the area of west Limerick and Kerry for the first few weeks of August before crossing over the Shannon to Clare, some credible evidence providing a taste of his rain-sodden peregrinations.

According to O'Gorman's own account, the 'people began by degrees to fall away from me' after the failure of Ballingarry. Then, 'a panic took place and I found myself isolated and in danger of arrest from hour to hour'. O'Gorman, John O'Donnell and Daniel Doyle spent the next few weeks travelling furtively around west Limerick and Kerry, taking shelter where they could in the homes of sympathisers, resting up and drying off. The parish priest of Abbeyfeale, who had opposed the Young Irelanders, harangued his parishioners and cast doubt on their motives, insisting that those who had 'rushed quickly enough to attack the mail coach' would 'rush even more quickly for the sake of the £2 or £3 you will get to betray each other'.[22] Fr Liddy was wrong, however, and the people in the main – though they might have been frightened of abetting the fugitives – did not refuse them food or shelter. This is clear from the fact that so many Young Irelanders with prices on their heads managed to flee the country. Those who *were* caught, such as Smith O'Brien and Meagher, were not taken as the result of betrayal.

There were, nonetheless, some penurious examples of young men willing to talk to the police in exchange for a few shillings; a statement from Maurice Dooley, a farm servant in Garryduff, provides a plausible and unembroidered account of O'Gorman's wanderings in west Limerick. It was eight o'clock on the evening of 4 August when three gentlemen arrived at the house of Patrick Corbett, Dooley's employer, about two miles from Newcastle West. 'They were very tired and their clothes were wet from per-spiration. One of them took off his shirt and gave it to me to get dried. Another of them got his stockings washed in the house.' Dooley was certain one of the men was O'Gorman, whom he had seen 'making a speech at Newcastle'. The men sent Dooley to another house in the area, where one of them had forgot-ten his cravat. When he returned, they dressed themselves and asked him to accompany them as a guide. They walked 'along the new mountain roads' until they came close to Ardagh, and then 'kept to the fields and went on in the same direction till we came near the River Shannon close to Askeaton'. One of the three men gave Dooley the gift of 'a pair of shoes', and they lay down to sleep in a cornfield near the Shannon 'and desired me to watch whilst they were sleeping'. Dooley 'got a lighted Coal to them from a house near[by] when they were resting to light their pipes ... They had pistols,' he told Inspector J.J. Kennedy and 'said they expected to find a boat to take them off'.[23]

Another informant, John O'Donahue, a farm labourer, described spending a night in the house of John Carmody, a large farmer in the parish of Cloneagh. O'Donahue testified to Kennedy that he heard a servant boy, Michael Sullivan, say 'that Richard O'Gorman had stopped in Carmody's house for several nights until Carmody got in dread of his remaining longer there'. O'Donahue made his mark with an *X*, acknowledging himself 'bound to our Sovereign Lady the Queen in the sum of Ten pounds to prosecute this information when called on'.[24]

A month later, following reports of illegal drilling, police searching houses in the area, including Carmody's, found 'a very handsome & well appointed dressing case … which must have been the property of a gentleman', the inference being that it was O'Gorman's. 'A very handsome & fashionable coat was also found which Head Constable Mills positively states he saw worn by O'Donnell, Solicitor of Limerick, who is now on the run.' Carmody was arrested a few days later.[25]

O'Gorman, O'Donnell and Doyle had by this stage made their way into County Clare, perhaps as early as Tuesday 8 August. Patrick Nash and James Dillane, both boatmen, were arrested a couple of days after this date for assisting the fugitives. According to Nash and Dillane 'a person of gentlemanly appearance' had paid them 'a sovereign' to carry him and two others from the shore of Foynes to the *Garryowen* steamer bound for Kilrush. The gentleman was 'a perfect stranger', they said, and they 'did not hesitate to earn the money'. Following this, there was a switch in focus to Clare in the search for

O'Gorman, and on Saturday 12 August a magistrate named Little, in the company of police and soldiers, made a vigorous search of all the hotels in Kilkee. The 'traitors' were once again said to be disguised as women, which meant the bedrooms of women were examined, 'notwithstanding the high rank of some'. This 'painful duty (as many of the ladies were in their beds) was performed by Mr Little alone, and in the most delicate manner possible, consistent with his magisterial duty'.[26]

The exact date of O'Gorman's crossing into Clare is uncertain. His discovery that 'the news of O'Brien's arrest had completely extinguished any spirit that [had] existed among the people there' is more clear-cut. The three fugitives concealed themselves as best they could, 'hoping against hope, that something might still happen, which would give us [a] means of retrieving the ruin in which our projects had become involved'. After a short period, however, they discovered that Doheny, Dillon and several others had already escaped to America, and that 'the insurrectionary movement was quite at an end'. The three comrades had endured 'much disappointment, much fatigue, hardship and misery'. They had trudged about in heavy rains that were laying the basis for another disastrous harvest and continued starvation. They had been 'hunted from place to place and forced to hide in wretched shelter'.[27] They decided to seek their own escape from Ireland – but how?

Fr Michael Meehan was a thirty-eight-year-old curate in the parish of Kilrush. A staunch nationalist from an early age, he had helped Daniel O'Connell during the famous Clare election of 1828. He went to Maynooth to study for the priest-hood the following year, and was a contemporary of Fr John Kenyon. In August 1848 he became the saviour of O'Gorman – whose shoes were 'torn and kept together by twine' – finding him shelter at the home of Dick Brew, a Protestant farmer. O'Gorman and his companions were hidden away for almost a month before an amenable ship's captain could be found. They were rowed out with muffled oars to a ship – named, ironically, the *Victoria and Albert* – by Meehan, Brew and one other. The rebels handed over £300 worth of gold, and were finally free and out to sea.[28]

A 'LINGERING POLITICAL DISCONTENT'

By the end of August 1848 the principal leaders of the Young Ireland movement were all either incarcerated or in flight. The mood of disaffection, however, was far from quelled. John O'Mahony, a large farmer in Tipperary and future Fenian, was particularly active, leading a series of guerrilla attacks on police barracks along the valley of the Suir throughout September. There were also rumours of an outbreak during Smith O'Brien's trial in Clonmel. The *Limerick Reporter* sensed this renewed spirit of insurrection, the 'tocsin of rebellion' sounding in 'every part of the country', the 'murmur of discontent … finding utterance on every lip … The harassed farmer – the unemployed artisan – the ejected tenants – the half-starved labourer – all seemed influenced by the same spirit, and are acting accordingly.'[29]

West Limerick, too, continued to show a remarkably strong streak of disorder, a lingering political discontent combining with the general disaffection that had always made it a centre of agrarian crimes, from the Whiteboys to the Rockites to the Terry Alts. An attack by insurgents on a small village near Rathkeale apparently left a poor-law officer seriously wounded. Michael Galway had information 'from respectable sources' that O'Gorman had returned to the locality 'and has joined the Insurgents who have fled to the Mountains after the late affair here'. They were, he believed, 'endeavouring to have another outbreak', and he asked for an entire company of infantry to be stationed in Abbeyfeale until the following spring, his area 'being the Key to Three Counties, Cork, Kerry & Limerick, & the badly disposed of either can be here in Two hours'.[30]

Galway was wrong about O'Gorman returning to Abbeyfeale but might have been correct about the rebellious mood re-emerging. In a second meeting with Inspector J.J. Kennedy of Newcastle West, John O'Donahue – the labourer who had already informed on John Carmody – described a night at the farm of Michael Costello. It was the evening of Sunday 17 September, just after sunset, 'when one of Costello's men came into the house and told us to come out and see the sight, that they were in Camp on the Mount!' O'Donahue left the house with Costello's wife and a few others. They crossed a field and saw about 200 men with firearms being drilled by Daniel Harnett and John Carmody, Harnett outlining to Carmody how 'he expected a French Officer before Friday or Saturday to command them'. Costello came home two hours later and was confronted by his wife, who said 'it would have been fitter for them all to be at home minding their own business'. Costello apparently replied 'that he would kick her if she did not mind what she said'. O'Donahue then 'supped' with Costello and 'in talking after supper as we were smoking' was told of a planned attack on Abbeyfeale the following week.[31]

Stories of O'Gorman stalking the hills of west Limerick with a band of 700 wild followers were utterly untrue. The authorities, however, were genuinely concerned about the reports of a rebel camp forming for an attack on Abbeyfeale – 'on Monday or Tuesday next' – even if O'Donahue had over-estimated the numbers. Sub-Inspector Graham of Newcastle West was in little doubt 'that "Danny Dan" is about here "Fraternising", and that we will have another shine'. Galway, determined to prevent 'another shine', brought extra soldiers into Abbeyfeale from surrounding towns. In the meantime, Kennedy – who felt O'Donahue's testimony was substantiated by other reports – had a number of the main protagonists arrested in advance of any action, including Costello and Carmody. In the event, 'everything passed off quietly' on the day of the expected attack, Galway certain his extra troops had 'struck terror' into the populace.[32]

Limerick city also experienced a minor, second wave of disturbances in late September, around the time of the Young Ireland trials, with two young men 'of respectable appearance' calling on Fr McMahon of Clonlara, County Clare, to ask 'what assistance they might expect from his parish as a general outbreak was intend[ed] to take place in Limerick on next Saturday night'. The priest did not think that his parishioners were inclined 'to join in any movement of the kind', but said 'that if they met him in Limerick on tomorrow in the shop of Corbet the grocer in Patrick Street he would be able to give them the information they required'. The naive young men, still clearly beholden to priests, agreed to meet him at noon. McMahon then went immediately to the police and offered to point out the men in the shop.[33]

It is not known if the priest followed through on his offer, but a young blacksmith named Thady O'Keefe was arrested a few days later for planning a rising. O'Keefe, a member of the old Sarsfield Club, had been heavily involved in protecting John Mitchel on the night of the riot in April. He was released quickly, however, as the authorities no longer expected any real threat. Other prisoners followed him out during the next few months, and in late November William Fuller Hartnett – the former president of the Felon Club in Newcastle West – became the last of the political prisoners to be released from Limerick Gaol. The authorities were so confident of their position by the end of the year that Caleb Powell was even able to secure a promise that no action would be taken if Daniel Doyle decided to return home from his hiding place.[34]

8

'THE EXILE'S LOT'

On Saturday 7 October 1848, a calm and unrepentant William Smith O'Brien was found guilty of high treason at a courtroom in Clonmel, County Tipperary. Two days later, three judges cowled in black caps sentenced him to death. His fellow prisoners, Thomas Francis Meagher, Terence Bellew MacManus and Patrick O'Donohoe, who had all been brought down from Kilmainham, quickly met with the same fate. There was no appetite in British government circles, however, to exact such severe retribution or to create martyrs. It was made clear from an early stage that the sentences would be commuted to transportation for life.

A series of legal disputes delayed the exile of the four Young Irelanders, and they reposed several months in well-appointed rooms in Richmond Prison. For Smith O'Brien – writing poetry in his comfortable cell and visited constantly by family and friends – these months of incarceration were 'one of the happiest periods of my life'. By contrast, John Martin and Kevin O'Doherty – convicted like John Mitchel on the lesser charge of treason-felony – were swiftly transported for ten years, the former describing in a letter from Cobh how they were forced to 'take the rations of the ordinary convicts ... or "arrange" with the Captain for a different mess'.[1] Charles Gavan Duffy, despite being tried five times, was eventually acquitted in April 1849. He restarted the *Nation* later that year, but grew disillusioned with Irish politics and left for Australia in 1855, rising through the ranks of the state legis-lature until he became prime minister of Victoria in June 1871. He was even knighted in 1873.

An emotional Smith O'Brien was finally forced to take leave of his family on 9 June 1849, boarding the *Swift* in Kingstown (Dún Laoghaire) alongside Meagher, MacManus and O'Donohoe – all bound for Van Diemen's Land. The prison colony had been receiving prisoners since 1803, including almost 1,000 men and women from Limerick: arsonists, prostitutes and thieves.[2] This system, however, was in its final stages by the time the Irish rebels arrived in October 1849, following a long-running campaign to abolish transportation to the island.

The authorities at Van Diemen's Land operated a ticket-of-leave system for certain higher-grade prisoners. The Irish rebels – far removed from the ordinary criminals who made up the bulk of the island's convict population – were offered these tickets-of-leave, whereby they were granted a large degree of freedom in exchange for a promise (or parole) not to escape. Smith O'Brien alone refused and was dispatched to the harsher environs of Maria Island and, later, Port Arthur. He endured a year of solitude and privations, and made one half-hearted effort to escape. The repeated urgings of family and friends finally convinced him, in November 1850, to accept a ticket-of-leave.

Smith O'Brien settled in the town of New Norfolk on the south of the island, taking a room at an inn that was paid for by rents from Cahirmoyle (much reduced on account of the Famine), which were collected and sent over by his younger brother Robert. Smith O'Brien rode horses, read prodigiously and befriended a number of local families, with whom he spent holidays and weekends. He was also close to some Catholic priests, which made his mother uneasy and fearful that he might convert. It was a lifestyle far removed from that of the less-privileged Irish convicts endlessly breaking stones in chain gangs. It was also a world away from the fate of captured rebels throughout Europe, thousands of whom were summarily shot on the battlefields of Hungary and Italy.

The move to New Norfolk enabled Smith O'Brien to meet up surreptitiously with the other Young Irelanders on the island, including Martin, O'Doherty and Mitchel, the latter having been transferred from Bermuda on account of his poor health. Mitchel, in contrast with the other exiles, arranged for his family to travel to Van Diemen's Land and he took up farming at Nant Cottage, near the quiet inland village of Bothwell. The family's passage was paid for in part by a sale of household goods just weeks after his conviction. A piano, two large bookcases, carpets, rugs, twelve mahogany chairs and more than 200 books had all been put up for sale. The auction in Rathmines received a great deal of attention, with many people travelling over fifty miles to buy 'some relic of this patriotic Irishman'.[3]

THE 'FIRST TO GET AWAY'

The various means of escape from Van Diemen's Land featured prominently in discussions among the exiles, and in February 1851 the ebullient and energetic MacManus became the first to get away, boarding a ship for the west coast of America just days after attending the ill-starred wedding of Meagher and a local girl named Catherine Bennett. MacManus arrived in San Francisco in early June and became the centre of week-long celebrations. He tried to set up as a shipping agent again, and even sent a business card to the governor of Van Diemen's Land.[4] Later, he turned to ranching in San Jose. He died an unrepentant rebel in January 1861, his funeral transformed by the Fenian Brotherhood into a great political set piece that saw his body carried back for burial in Ireland.

Meagher followed MacManus' example in January 1852, even boarding the same vessel, the *Elizabeth Thompson*, leaving behind a heavily pregnant young wife and with some unease about his escape, due to the terms of his ticket-of-leave. The iconic 'Meagher of the Sword' was the most celebrated of all the Young Ireland rebels in America. He embarked on a series of profitable speaking tours, but seemed dissatisfied and unfulfilled, moving quickly between lecturing, newspapers and the law. His infant son died in Van Diemen's Land without Meagher ever seeing him. His wife then came to live with him in New York, but the marriage was troubled and she moved to Ireland to live with Meagher's family. She died in Waterford in May 1854, just twenty-two years old and a month after giving birth to a second boy. Meagher became 'an edgy presence in the Manhattan streets'. A year later, he made a more auspicious marriage, to Elizabeth Townsend, the daughter of a well-connected New York business family. The American Civil War finally provided the grand stage Meagher's ego and personality demanded. He led the Irish Brigade in a number of important battles, including Fredericksburg, and was made a general of the Union army. After the war he went to Montana, where he drowned in tragic, somewhat mysterious circum-stances.[5]

There were no qualms about any breach of parole when a depressed and dispirited Patrick O'Donohoe fled Van Diemen's Land in November 1852. Upon arrival in the colony, he had established a newspaper, the *Irish Exile*, but had then fallen foul of the authorities, losing his ticket-of-leave on a number of occasions, being forced into hard labour with the common convicts and being locked up at night 'with the vilest of the vile' and 'covered with vermin until four o'clock the following morning'.[6] In America, he fared little better. He did not receive the lavish honours bestowed on Meagher and died in January 1854 on the very morning his wife and family arrived from Ireland. He was already dead in his Brooklyn lodgings when they found him, his health broken by excessive drinking and captivity.

John Mitchel was the last of the Young Irelanders to escape, sailing like the others to America, where he was rapturously received in late 1853. He established a newspaper in New York called the *Citizen*, which proved instantly controversial. He moved to Tennessee, where he first farmed and then edited another newspaper, the *Southern Citizen*. In later years, Mitchel worked as a financial agent for the Fenians in Paris, and even returned to Ireland in the mid-1870s. He was elected an MP for County Tipperary in 1875, just a month before he died, but was declared ineligible. His post-1848 life is best known, however, for his strong advocacy of slavery and vociferous support of the South during the American Civil War, two interlinked views that brought him notoriety but must also be seen in the context of his deep hatred for the capitalist systems of England and North America.[7]

In early 1854 the remaining Young Irelanders in exile – Smith O'Brien, O'Doherty and Martin – were granted conditional pardons by the British government, allowing them to return to Europe, but not Britain or Ireland. This was, in part, the result of petitions for clemency, but was also a conciliatory gesture on the eve of the Crimean War, for which Irish soldiers would be required to fight in the British army. Smith O'Brien was delighted, of course, particularly as he was not called upon to 'make application for it in some form or other' or 'say or write or do anything which could be interpreted as a confession on my part that I consider myself a "criminal" in regard of the transactions of 1848'. Nevertheless, he still felt somewhat lost and restless, like a man 'without a home, a wanderer on the Face of the Earth'.[8]

In July 1856, a full pardon having been granted by Queen Victoria to celebrate the end of the Crimean War, William Smith O'Brien left Brussels, where he had been living, to return to Ireland. Kevin O'Doherty and John Martin also received full pardons. Great fires lit O'Brien's journey home to Cahirmoyle. His mother, Lady O'Brien, wrote to Lord Palmerston, the prime minister, offering her thanks for her son's return 'to his native land', and even promised he would be 'entirely separated from his former Political Companions'. Smith O'Brien was not quietened so easily. He took on the role of an elder statesman, and published numerous pamphlets and articles on political affairs. His last years, however, were devoted more to European travel than Irish politics. He died in Wales in June 1864, three years after his wife. His funeral, according to local newspapers, was among the largest ever seen in the county, the cortège two miles long and composed not just of the gentry but all the peasantry of the area. Smith O'Brien's own tenants had earlier kissed the lid of his coffin as it lay in state in a room in Cahirmoyle.[9]

YOUNG IRELAND ÉMIGRÉS

On Tuesday 31 October 1848, a 'very weather-beaten and thin' John Blake Dillon arrived at the New York hotel room of his brother-in-law Charles Hart, a Young Irelander who had fled to America that July. Dillon, like Richard O'Gorman and Meagher, had been sheltered after the rising by friendly priests in the west of Ireland. He then shaved off his prominent sideburns and, adopting the disguise of a priest, boarded a brig, the *Gem*, in Galway Bay and set sail for America.[10] Another Young Irelander, P.J. Smyth, also escaped on the same ship. They were joined in New York by an incredible influx of Young Ireland émigrés, including John Savage, Thomas Antisell, James Cantwell, John Kavanagh and innumerable minor members of the movement. They were, however, just a fraction of the 90,000 Irish immigrants to disembark in New York in 1848, the Famine exodus transforming the face of that city forever.

Dillon was accepted immediately into the hearts and homes of Irish-American luminaries such as Charles O'Conor and Robert Emmet, a grandson of Thomas Addis Emmet, brother of the executed martyr Robert Emmet. Dillon was dining with the Emmets one night when 'who should walk in but T[homas] D[evin] Reilly, just landed, greatly reduced by his adventures and voyage'.[11] The night was spent enjoyably, Reilly regaling his audience with a comical account of his escape. Reilly, however, was much more militant than Dillon and quickly launched a radical newspaper called the *People*, which folded after six months. He then worked for an assortment of publications, including the *Democratic Review*, the *American Review* and, in Boston (where he married Jennie Miller, from

County Fermanagh), a labour paper, the *Protective Union*. He died a few weeks before his thirtieth birthday, in 1854, his passing mourned in verse by his friend Joseph Brenan's 'Dirge on O'Reilly'.

The redoubtable Michael Doheny was the next Young Irelander to have his arrival in America noted by Hart. He had escaped from Ireland dressed as a farmer, making his way from Cork to Bristol to Paris. He reached New York in early 1849, walking into Mass one Sunday morning 'blooming after a sojourn in France and a long sea voyage', and bumping into Dillon and Hart. Doheny set to work on his *Felon's Track*, which was published later that year. His mind still filled with images of rebellion, he began to organise militia companies in New York in the vain hope of some future invasion of Ireland. He was later involved in the establishment of the Fenian Brotherhood with John O'Mahony and James Stephens, and, in 1861, accompanied Terence Bellew MacManus' remains back to Ireland. He returned to America, where he took a small part in the Civil War before dying in April 1862.[12]

Relations between the Young Irelanders in America were often strained, factions forming between the moderates such as Dillon and the militants like Doheny and Reilly. Thomas D'Arcy McGee, however, was the only exile to be truly ostracised by the group, as Dillon made clear in his correspondence with Smith O'Brien.[13] McGee, who had lived in America in the early 1840s, made a lot of enemies upon his return there with his abusive writings. He later transformed into a rabidly pro-Catholic, anti-

Fenian politician in Canada. He was assassinated in April 1868, possibly by Fenians who considered him a traitor to the Irish cause.

'FREE AND ABLE TO ROAM'

While the majority of Young Irelanders fled immediately to America or France, Richard O'Gorman, for a short period at least, 'found Christian shelter under the crescent of the Turk', his precarious adventures in Limerick and Clare finally ending with a ship's voyage to Istanbul. O'Gorman's next move was to contact the French general and politician Louis Cavaignac (who he may have known during his stint with the National Guard) to secure passports and a passage to France.[14]

O'Gorman was definitely in Paris by 16 January 1849, the date he composed a long and often despairing letter to a then still imprisoned Smith O'Brien. Deploring the 'miserable' state of Irish society, O'Gorman felt certain that Smith O'Brien had done 'all that men could do to raise the heart of Ireland'. It was not his fault the country had failed him 'in the hour of need'. O'Gorman was clearly still furious with the Old Irelanders, a 'crew of cowards and hucksters', who he blamed, at least in part, for the failed rising. The country, it appeared to his jaundiced eyes, preferred 'corruption and falsehood' to 'honour and worth'. 'If so', he concluded bitterly, 'it deserves the curse that rests upon it, and God's will be done'.

O'Gorman's mood lifted in the latter part of the letter. He

had been well received by the Irish community in Paris and had just seen Miles Byrne, the elderly United Irishman, who was 'as full as ever of love for his old home and of sympathy and respect for you and the other victims of our unfortunate attempt'. He sketched out the political scene in France, where Louis Napoleon, a nephew of the great emperor, had just been elected president. Of his own travails in getting out of Ireland, he merely stated they were 'so many and so strange, that even to myself, they seem more like some tale of fiction than real stubborn truth'.[15]

O'Gorman was back in touch with Smith O'Brien four months later, this time from Bruges. He apologised for being so slow in his reply to a letter of Smith O'Brien's, and pleaded a guilty conscience at being free and able to roam about and enjoy the sights of Europe. He was with his parents and 'many a time when we felt the free air of the Rhine blowing on our cheeks, we said from our hearts – would to God, *they* were here'. O'Gorman, who was preparing to sail to America, speculated upon his future there. He did not want the role of a mere 'Irish agitator' but wished instead to work hard and raise by his own conduct 'the character of our little Band'. Then he could write no more: 'my heart is very full and thoughts are crowding fast'. He wished only that Smith O'Brien could be free.[16]

O'Gorman set sail from Le Havre on the morning of 1 June 1849, arriving in America just in time for Independence Day. He lived in St Louis, Missouri, for almost a year before settling down in New York. He was admitted to the New York bar and went into partnership with Dillon, the two Young Irelanders living and working together in Brooklyn. O'Gorman's parents travelled over at the beginning of 1852 and spent most of the year living with their son in New York.[17]

O'Gorman – an articulate and well-bred Irish rebel – had immediate prestige in New York, and became a figurehead of fraternal organisations such as the Society of the Friendly Sons of St Patrick. He stood on innumerable platforms to deliver speeches on Ireland and America, on history, politics and literature, becoming in the process 'a supreme example of an idealistic Irish revolutionary turned pragmatic American politico'. He was far removed from the likes of Doheny and O'Mahony, who immersed themselves in secret societies. To agitators like the Fenian John O'Leary, he was just a pageant speech-maker who had 'exhausted his whole stock of patriotism in '48', someone who took 'little part in Irish affairs' thereafter, 'save in what may be called the ornamental [St] Patrick's day line of business'. James Stephens called him a 'fat greasy bourgeois' who had made a fortune from his connection to 1848.[18]

Dillon went back to Ireland in May 1856 as part of the general amnesty to mark the conclusion of the Crimean War. He stayed aloof from Irish politics at first, but was later elected an MP for Tipperary. O'Gorman, who had married an American, chose to remain in New York, where he prospered in business, politics and society. He forged links with New York's elite, and watched his law practice grow to become one of the most 'extensive and lucrative' in the city. Another letter to Smith O'Brien described how 'I like it [America] extremely, because I suppose, it likes me'. He returned to Dublin briefly in the summer of 1859 and was received warmly by the people of the city.[19]

Writing to Smith O'Brien on the first day of 1859, O'Gorman depicted American politics as 'a filthy pool of shabbiness falsehood and corruption'.[20] It was not long, however, before the Young Irelander was caught up in that mire, aligning himself with the infamously corrupt William 'Boss' Tweed of Tammany Hall, the dominant figure in New York politics during the 1860s. O'Gorman was elevated to the important position of corporation counsel and earned a highly improper fortune as Tweed plundered the coffers of the city. Tweed's reign of corruption was ended by a court case in 1871, and though O'Gorman was implicated in the various frauds, he escaped censure. He overcame this discreditable episode and was even elected a Superior Court judge in New York in 1882. He died in early 1895, the obituary in the *New York Times* remembering him as a 'distinguished jurist and orator'.[21]

O'Gorman's deep involvement with the 'Tweed Ring' raises uncomfortable questions about his character and choices in America. Nevertheless, the accusations of O'Leary and others – which have sullied O'Gorman's reputation – lack balance. O'Gorman was the refined, well-educated son of an affluent Dublin businessman. A fine career in law and a high position in society lay before him in Dublin. He gave it away in 1848 when swept up by the intoxicant of revolution. New York offered a second chance at the kind of life he had seemed destined for as a young man, and he, not unnaturally, seized the opportunity. Assessments of O'Gorman must acknowledge that he had served the Irish cause well enough when traversing the diseased, rain-sodden fields of west Limerick, a price on his head and no guarantee of success in the future.

Looking back on Young Ireland and 1848 (from a distance of thousands of miles and more than thirty years), O'Gorman regretted that the French revolution had 'hurried on events before their time'. The Young Irelanders, he believed, would have been better off concentrating on their first stated cause: 'the social and political education of the Irish people'. He was nonetheless proud of the men and women whose fortunes he shared, young people 'who flung into the movement the treasures of their intellects and their hopes'. He was proud 'to have taken part in their counsels', and 'even to have shared their defeat'. They had, he felt, sustained the reputation of 'Irish intellect' and 'Irish patriotism'.[22]

'MY OWN LOST NATIVE LAND'

Daniel 'Danny Dan' Harnett, the 'insurgent chief' of Abbeyfeale, escaped the wilds of west Limerick and Kerry 'in the garb of a Friar', alighting first at Paris before continuing on to America, a familiar route for the Irish rebels. A few years later, he was among those invited to attend a ball in New York to celebrate the second anniversary of Meagher's escape from Van Diemen's Land.[23] The party was held at an Irish theatre called Niblo's.

Bartholomew Dowling, the poet of the Sarsfield Club, also moved to America, settling down in California in the early 1850s and playing host to MacManus and Mitchel when they arrived in the state. He worked at first in mining and farming before becoming editor of the *San Francisco Monitor* in 1858. He also continued to write poetry, including 'The Foreign Shamrock', one melancholic verse of which ran thus:

> I place the leaves above my heart, as a wondrous talis-
> man,
> For they bear me back to a better time, ere the exile's lot
> began;
> And again, in the flush of glowing youth, among my own
> I stand,
> In the bright mirage of a generous hope, in my own lost
> native land.

Dowling died, unmarried, in 1863 at the age of forty.[24]

John McClenahan was another Limerick confederate to seek refuge in America – exiled, according to his old newspaper, 'for loving Ireland too well'. McClenahan was better prepared than many other political refugees. With no warrant out for his arrest, he had been able to get some affairs in order, and arrived in New York with a bag full of references from priests, including Fr Kenyon. He also carried with him a letter of introduction from Duffy dated 'Newgate Prison, Aug. 6, 1848', which read:

> My Dear —, The bearer of this note, Mr McClenahan, editor of the *Limerick Reporter*, desires an introduction to you. He was a zealous confederate and an accomplished journalist, who did good service to the country which he only abandoned because he believes he can be of no more service to it for the present.[25]

McClenahan arrived in America aboard the same ship as Thomas Antisell, a Dublin confederate who went on to work as a scientist for the American government. McClenahan's first venture in his new homeland was the reproduction of portraits of the Young Irelanders. Charles Hart bought one of the pictures of Smith O'Brien and hung it in his hotel room in New York. The former editor then turned his attention back to journalism and was involved in the launch of the *People* with Devin Reilly.[26] He worked on a number of other newspapers before joining Mitchel on the *Citizen* in 1854. When Mitchel left a year later, McClenahan took over as proprietor and editor.

McClenahan, regrettably, was not immune to the faction-alism that blighted the Irish-American community in New York. He became embroiled in a dispute with Doheny around the time of the Crimean War, a period of heightened tensions among Irish-American revolutionaries. Both men saw England's involvement in a war with Russia as an opportunity for revolution in Ireland. They belonged, however, to rival organisations vying for the support of Irish-American New York. McClenahan's *Citizen* was the mouthpiece of the Irish Emigrant Aid Society, a benevolent-sounding organisation nonetheless pledged to the liberation of Ireland. Doheny, meanwhile, was a founding member of the secretive Emmet Monument Association, a forerunner of the Fenian Brotherhood. The two groups spent more time denigrating each other than working towards any action in Ireland, Doheny even accusing McClenahan of being an English spy. McClenahan died a few years later, not long before the marriages of his two daughters, Carrie and Lizzie, in the mid-1860s.[27]

Daniel Doyle, McClenahan's co-conspirator from the year of revolutions, returned to Limerick in October 1849. Two months earlier, Queen Victoria had paid a triumphant visit to the country, and with Ireland proving loyal and tranquil, the authorities turned a blind eye to the reappearance of wanted men, notwithstanding one last Young Ireland outbreak in September, an abortive attack on the police barracks in Cappoquin led by the remnants of the movement, including James Fintan Lalor and Joseph Brenan. Doyle might have been able to return even earlier, Caleb Powell having secured an 'official assurance' guaranteeing his safety in December 1848. He does not seem to have trusted this assurance, however, and stayed hidden a good deal longer. John O'Donnell, Doyle's old Sarsfield Club companion, followed him back to Limerick a few weeks later, returning to work very quickly and attending the petty sessions, where he was 'congratulated by his friends in court'.[28]

Doyle had been on the run with O'Gorman in west Limerick but did not escape with him. He remained in Ireland for some time, and Duffy has described him visiting Smith O'Brien in 1849, 'walking in and out of the prison at discretion, under a feigned name', the authorities certain he had absconded to Istanbul. Doheny's description of Doyle escaping 'across the water' suggests he went no further than England during his absence from home. O'Donnell, on the other hand, definitely fled the country with O'Gorman, living in Paris for a number of months and encountering John O'Mahony and other exiles.[29]

O'Donnell and Doyle were both active in Limerick society during the more prosperous years of the 1850s. They went back to work as solicitors, with offices, respectively, at 62 William Street and 41 Cecil Street. They were among the first donors to the Limerick Athenaeum, an establishment founded in 1856 to encourage literary and scientific learning by another erstwhile Young Irelander, William Lane Joynt. Other subscribers to this fund included old friends like Kenyon and old foes like Henry Maunsell, the sheriff in Limerick city during 1848. They also maintained a strong interest in local politics, and served as town councillors.[30]

O'Donnell continued to work as an election agent for a number of parliamentary candidates in Limerick city, including, in 1858, the timber magnate James Spaight. A year later, however, he switched sides and helped a Major George Gavin run against Spaight. Gavin was elected but Spaight challenged the result, accusing O'Donnell of having organised a mob to disturb the polling and intimidate voters. An inquiry was held in the city, with a number of prominent witnesses called to give evidence. O'Donnell was assisted by the testimony of the resident magistrate, Pierce George Barron, an old adversary from 1848. Barron admitted that there had been some trouble and the throwing of stones at voters. Nevertheless, it had, in his opinion, been one of the quietest elections during his twelve years in Limerick. The committee investigating the result found no evidence against Gavin or his agents and O'Donnell's candidate kept his seat in the Westminster parliament.[31]

O'Donnell – who, of the two friends, was the more interested in nationalist politics after 1848 – was among the thousands of mourners to follow MacManus' coffin through the streets of Cork in 1861 after the ship carrying his remains landed in Ireland. Both O'Donnell and Doyle attended Smith O'Brien's funeral in 1864. A year later, they were chosen as members of a committee set up to raise a monument to Smith O'Brien, a feat achieved just six years later when a statue to the Young Irelander went up in Dublin. Other members of this committee included John Blake Dillon, William Fuller Hartnett – the old confederate and businessman from Newcastle West – Isaac Butt, the Home Ruler, and Maurice Lenihan, the journalist who had purchased the *Limerick Reporter* in 1850.[32]

O'Donnell, who had been in poor health for a number of years, died a year before the statue was unveiled. It was said locally that his regular illnesses had all originated in the hardships he had endured in 1848 when a 'high-spirited and active Young Irelander of the school of O'Brien and Meagher'. O'Donnell died aged fifty-one and was buried at Mount St Lawrence cemetery in Limerick city. His son and Daniel Doyle were among the chief mourners. He was remembered by the *Nation* as 'a man of pure heart, of brilliant intellect, and of generous soul', one of 'the illustrious proscribed in the days of Forty-Eight'.[33]

Daniel Doyle, a father of six, followed O'Donnell to the grave four years later and was, in fact, buried alongside his old friend. His death was much more of a shock to their friends in Limerick. O'Gorman, in his reminiscences, wrote of them fondly as two men 'whose courage, fidelity, endurance, [and] gallant and unselfish patriotism' he would 'never fail to remember with affection and respect'.[34]

9

'This cursed Ballingarry'

The English novelist William Makepeace Thackeray was holidaying in the Belgian resort town of Spa when, on the morning of Friday 11 August 1848, a waiter delivered to his room a letter from home and a copy of *The Times*. Thackeray, who had just 'finished writing page seven' of his novel *Pendennis*, put the letter to one side and turned quickly to *The Times*, the mighty organ of upper middle-class England. Soon absorbed in its pages, he read with glee how the 'deplorable revolution and rebellion' in Ireland had been 'averted in so singular, I may say unprecedented a manner'. The author thrilled at the 'pitiful … figure cut by Mr Smith O'Brien, and indeed by Popery altogether!'[1]

Rehearsing tactics employed against the Chartists, *The Times* had built up in the weeks before the rebellion the threat posed by the Young Irelanders and then laughed at its demise. In a series of columns entitled 'The insurrectionary movement', its correspondents described Galway as 'a nest of clubs' and declared County Louth to be in the midst of a 'pike and rifle mania'. Carrick-on-Suir was inhabited 'by a wild and lawless race, ripe for any scheme, however desperate'. The editorials were equally severe, calling the Young Irelanders 'Jacobin, Republican and Communist'. An Irish rebellion, the newspaper promised, would lead to 'massacre, revenge, plunder, wanton destruction, the blackened walls of mansions and factories' and 'ships burning in the docks'. Inflammatory reports of that ilk had swelled the ranks of 'special constables' in early April. The articles on Ireland – for which Lord Clarendon thanked the editor – helped convince the government of the necessity of suspending habeas corpus.[2]

The tone of *The Times* was transformed by news of the failure at Ballingarry. Again mimicking its treatment of the Chartists after the mass rally in April, the newspaper switched from morbid fears to hysterical laughter. The rebellion, 'a great sham', was likened to a play that fails to open: 'when we looked for the curtain to arise, the lights were extinguished'. The Irish people, *The Times* opined, had proved themselves 'idiots and poltroons', whilst the 'rebel army was from head to tail one mass of imbecility'. William Smith O'Brien, 'more like Robinson Crusoe than the King of Munster', was subjected to a particularly cutting form of pitying contempt: 'Armed with pike and pistol, muttering broken sentences, and with a reckless swaggering gait, he goes he knows not whither, and does he knows not what.' A constant refrain in the coverage was the questioning of Smith O'Brien's very sanity: words such as 'mental condition', 'stray lunatic' and 'poor crazy rebel' were used in abundance.[3]

The cruellest passages in *The Times* portrayed a cowardly Smith O'Brien avoiding the fire of the police by 'crawling on all fours, like a tortoise, among the cabbages' of Widow McCormack's back garden. This derogatory image proved popular, and the newspaper returned to it often in the weeks and months following the rising. In the early 1850s Charles Gavan Duffy attacked *The Times* for having coined 'the "cabbage garden" lie in '48', but he could not shift it from the popular imagination. In 1862 Smith O'Brien even challenged Robert Peel, the son of the former prime minister, to a duel after a jibe about the 'cabbage garden heroes'. The *Evening Mail* responded to this news by suggesting they fight with cabbage stalks instead of pistols. Duffy, visiting Ireland from Australia, was on the defensive again in 1865 when a guest at a dinner party made a joke about Smith O'Brien and the cabbage patch. With John Blake Dillon and P.J. Smyth among the other diners, Duffy told the offender – a man named Prendergast – 'that if he wanted to disparage a generous gentleman, he ought to do so somewhere else than among that gentleman's intimate friends'.[4] Nevertheless, the image of Smith O'Brien's feeble stand in the cabbage patch has endured, a cruel axiom of Irish history despite the exertions of the Young Irelanders to imbue their exploits with at least some hint of glory.

A 'FUND OF TREASON AND DISAFFECTION'

When, following his conviction in May 1848, John Mitchel had been shipped across the Atlantic to the convict colony of Bermuda on the aptly named steamer the *Scourge*. Upon arrival he was transferred to the prison ship *Dromedary*. As a high-profile political prisoner, Mitchel was kept apart from, and treated far better than, the mass of the convicts. He was forbidden to read newspapers but this did not stop sympathetic guards from smuggling them into him. These newspapers were usually several weeks or even months old when passed on to Mitchel, and it was not until Tuesday 24 October 1848 that he discovered news of the 'poor extemporised abortion of a rising in Tipperary, headed by Smith O'Brien' at a place he called 'this cursed Ballinagarry [*sic*]'.[5]

Mitchel's initially harsh and derisive assessment of the rising, jotted down in the notebooks that formed the body of his famous *Jail Journal*, was tempered a few weeks later by news of the convictions for treason of Smith O'Brien and three other Young Irelanders. 'British dominion' in Ireland, he argued, had 'been damaged, and heavily' by the rebellion, a 'fund of treason and disaffection … laid up for future use'. The work of the Young Irelanders, 'with our *Nation*s, and our Irish libraries and ballads, and the rest of it' would bear fruit in years to come when the children of the Famine who had grown up amid talk of the Young Irelanders reached maturity. John Devoy – the Fenian born in the early 1840s and raised by a father who read the *Nation* aloud each night – would prove one striking example of this prophecy.[6] Michael Doheny was another Young Irelander to accentuate the positives in his post-rising writings – *The Felon's Track* much more a celebration of the movement than a lament.

The instant histories of Doheny and Mitchel (published in 1849 and 1854 respectively) were augmented through the years by the recollections of various Young Irelanders published in newspapers and larger narratives, such as John Savage's '98 and '48 (1856) and James E. McGee's *The Men of '48* (1881). There were also popular Young Ireland-themed novels, like Charles Kickham's *Knocknagow* (1879). It is no surprise that the rebellion has been termed 'a literary event'.[7] The Young Irelanders – poets and writers all – made themselves the first prodigious chroniclers of the movement, providing in the process a heady mix of self-glorification and score-settling, glorious prose, questionable conclusions and a strong antidote to the disparagements of *The Times*.

The pinnacle of these Young Ireland histories was Duffy's monumental two-volume account published in the early 1880s. *Young Ireland* (1880) and *Four Years of Irish History* (1883) were well received and were reissued at regular intervals. While far from impartial, the sheer scale of these books has left all historians of the period very deeply in Duffy's debt. Regarding Ballingarry, Duffy did not shy away from stark facts; it was 'a poor, feeble, unprosperous essay'. Nonetheless, he contended with pride, 'it was dignified and sublimated by the unflinching courage and devotion of the men engaged in it'. It was, he argued, no more heroic 'to stake life for the common weal at Thermopylae or Bannockburn' than at Ballingarry. The 'Cabbage Garden', he believed, would 'attract the sympathy and reverence of generous minds long after more successful achievements have been forgotten'.[8]

In 1898 the octogenarian Charles Gavan Duffy published another two-volume work, an autobiography entitled *My Life in Two Hemispheres*. Its publication was well timed to coincide with the fiftieth anniversary of the Young Ireland rising, but lacked 'the brilliance and coherence of his earlier writings'. Among the other books released around this time was a biography of the talented but troubled Young Ireland poet James Clarence Mangan, author of the haunting 'My Dark Rosaleen'. A number of articles were also produced on the Young Irelanders in nationalist journals such as *Shan Van Vocht*. The attention, however, visited upon the Young Irelanders and their rising paled in comparison to the centenary celebrations of the 1798 rebellion. These United Irishmen celebrations commenced on New Year's Eve 1897 with a series of torchlight parades through large cities including Dublin, Limerick and Cork.[9]

Throughout 1898 *Shan Van Vocht* carried advertisements for commemorative mementos, including Wolfe Tone brooches, United Irishmen pendants and '98 scarf pins. There were no William Smith O'Brien accessories. The martyrs Emmet and Tone, it is clear, were deemed more worthy of glorification than the transported Young Irelanders – the pikemen of Wexford effortlessly eclipsing in the public mind the apparently cowardly confederate clubmen of Tipperary, and the fierce fighting of Vinegar Hill a powerful antidote to the inglorious affair at

Ballingarry. The editors of *Shan Van Vocht* tried to raise the memory of Young Ireland to a similar plane, one article in February stating:

> And so whilst the memory of the men of '98 is in this Centenary year placed in the front, we would not have it forgotten that fifty years ago, half-way back across the century, men as true and determined wrote and wrought and suffered, and were ready to die for Ireland.

The efforts of the journal were in vain; a later article voiced disappointment that while the centenary celebrations had seen 'hill-fires all over the country' and a gathering of thousands on top of Vinegar Hill, yet 'we have heard not a word of the Young Irelanders, who fifty years ago in black '48, proved their love for their oppressed and famine-stricken country'.[10]

The overshadowing of the Young Irelanders in 1898 did not mean their influence was in total abeyance. The ballad poetry of Thomas Davis, Richard D'Alton Williams, James Clarence Mangan and others contributed immensely to the Gaelic Revival of the late nineteenth century. Canonical tomes like the *Jail Journal* continued to inspire Irish nationalists, constitutionalist and revolutionary alike, including several leaders of the 1916 Easter Rising. William Redmond, a brother of the Home Rule MP John Redmond, said reading the *Jail Journal* converted him to nationalism. John Dillon, the politician and son of a Young Irelander, was a more obvious devotee, his brother William authoring an impressive two-volume biography of Mitchel in the late 1880s. In 1906 Roger Casement read the *Jail Journal* while travelling to Brazil, admitting its impact stayed with him forever. Patrick Pearse called Mitchel one of 'the four apostles' of Irish nationalism, and placed 1848 very firmly in the line linking 1798 to his own 1916.[11]

Arthur Griffith, one of the negotiators of the 1921 Anglo-Irish Treaty, was perhaps the political leader most profoundly affected by the Young Irelanders. Having joined the literary Young Ireland Society while still a teenager, he won a prize for an essay in 1885, and was given a copy of Mitchel's *History of Ireland from the Treaty of Limerick*. A few months later, he delivered a paper on his new hero Mitchel to his branch of this new society in Upper Abbey Street, Dublin. Also around this time, Griffith encountered an elderly priest who caught him pulling a Union Jack down from a lamppost. The priest congratulated the young Griffith instead of chastising him, for Fr C.P. Meehan had been one of the men to follow Smith O'Brien out of Conciliation Hall that fateful night in 1846.[12] Griffith later established a journal that he called the *United Irishman* in conscious imitation of Mitchel. Griffith was a remarkably assiduous keeper of the Young Ireland flame during the years surrounding the 1916 Rising, publishing new versions of the *Jail Journal* and *The Felon's Track*, and editing collections of the writings of Thomas Davis and Thomas Meagher.

Elsewhere, the prominence James Connolly gave James Fintan Lalor in his *Labour in Irish History* led to the publication of a number of books on Lalor in the late 1910s. Mitchel, however, remained the most noted Young Irelander, even if he was often fêted and despised in equal measure. A review of a biography of Mitchel by the nationalist historian P.S. O'Hegarty praised the 'moral grandeur and intellectual strength' of his subject. One illustrious contemporary, the poet William Butler Yeats, was less enamoured of the 'rancorous, devil-possessed' writings of Mitchel, despite a lifelong friendship with the Fenian John O'Leary, a Young Ireland adherent in his youth.[13]

'EVOLUTION OF THE IRISH NATION'

In late November 1914, just weeks after the beginning of the First World War, Denis Gwynn – a young student at Trinity College, Dublin, and a great-grandson of William Smith O'Brien – chaired a meeting where Patrick Pearse discussed Wolfe Tone, and William Butler Yeats delivered a 'Tribute to Thomas Davis'. Thirty-five years later, Gwynn – now Professor of Modern Irish History at University College, Cork – published *Young Ireland and 1848*, the first major modern treatment of the movement. It was just one of a number of works to mark the complementary centennials of the death of Thomas Davis and the Young Ireland rebellion. M.J. MacManus, a journalist at the *Irish Press*, edited *Thomas Davis and Young Ireland* (1945), T.D. Sullivan, an old associate of Griffith's on the *United Irishman*, produced the still incredibly valuable biographical compendium *The Young Irelanders* (1944), and R.D. Edwards, one of the founders of the journal *Irish Historical Studies*, provided an influential essay entitled 'The Contribution of Young Ireland to the Development of the Irish National Idea'. The centenary, nevertheless, did not attract much public attention, and was overshadowed once again by commemorations of 1798 that included a massive parade through Dublin.[14]

Edwards' conclusion that the Young Ireland rebellion had been little more than a 'token insurrection' was balanced by an acknowledgement that the 'tradition of Young Ireland' had proven a 'powerful force in the evolution of the Irish nation'. This two-sided appraisal has held sway for fifty years, generations of historians ridiculing the rising as 'pathetic', a 'hopeless gesture' and a 'fiasco' while in the same breath confirming the far-reaching influence of the Young Irelanders, their 'legacy of ideas' including Mitchel's politicisation of the Famine, Davis' non-sectarianism, and Lalor's radical views on tenants' rights. The impact of the exiles on Irish-America has also been acknowledged as significant.[15]

Recent works on Young Ireland have dispensed with such loaded terms as 'pathetic', preferring instead carefully worded phrases like 'small and unsuccessful rising'. They have also attempted to shift the emphasis away from Ballingarry and back toward the intoxicating days of the 'springtime of peoples', highlighting the international dimensions to the movement and the extent to which it was seen as a real threat to the English state. This is where the real measure of the movement can be found, not Ballingarry.[16]

Writing in 1988, Richard Davis ended his important study of the Young Ireland movement with the observation that the 'Catholic-Protestant pluralism they advocated in theory and practised amongst themselves' was 'perhaps their finest legacy to Ireland at the end of the twentieth century'. This was a theme picked up in 1998 when the sesquicentennial celebrations occurred against a backdrop of the signing of the Good Friday Agreement: the explicitly non-sectarian nature of the movement chimed well with the mood of post-peace-process Ireland. Fittingly, it was announced that the 'Warhouse' – Widow McCormack's cottage – was to be purchased by the state and turned into a museum.[17] The museum opened in the summer of 2004.

LEGACY

Ballingarry was the signature event of 1848 in Ireland, the beginning and end of genuine hopes for armed rebellion, an ad-hoc, off-the-cuff engagement. It was a failure, unquestionably so. The leaders of the Young Ireland movement had roused men and women to the point of arms but then did not know quite what to do with them. They were beset by intractable problems, such as the Famine and the suspicions of the clergy, as well as many more of their own making. The revolution, however, was not a case of massive self-delusion. There were a number of related outbreaks, and Munster especially was far from devoid of martial spirit. Limerick was to the fore of these disturbances, the people of the west of the county in particular still inspired by the images of freedom and rebellion that had been glancing through their minds since springtime. Their actions were sporadic and uncoordinated, but strong – illegal – actions nonetheless. The hundreds of men and women involved were willing to risk death, injury or imprisonment. Even as winter approached and all hope seemed to have faded, they continued to provide for and hide their friends and neighbours on the run. Eight years later, during the summer of 1856, they rejoiced at the return of their favourite son, the hero/martyr William Smith O'Brien, a cordon of bonfires lighting his path all the way from Limerick city to Cahirmoyle.

Historians and protagonists alike have questioned whether the Young Ireland rebellion even deserves that lofty appellation 'rebellion'.[1] At first glance, they have a point. What happened in Ballingarry was a minor engagement, a skirmish with just two casualties, a far cry from the 30,000 deaths in 1798. It is the surrounding circumstances that raise Ballingarry to the level of revolt. Other 'constabulary affrays' in nineteenth-century Ireland did not occur against a backdrop of revolution surging through Europe, of months of seditious speeches by popular men of high profile, including an MP, or of the suspension of habeas corpus by a clearly anxious British government. Nor were those involved charged with high treason and sentenced to death. All the accoutrements and accessories of a rebellion were present, and weigh as heavily as the actual occurrences in Ballingarry. The Young Ireland rebellion is therefore deserving of that designation.

The peasants and colliers throwing stones at the police in Widow McCormack's house might not have thought of themselves as fully fledged rebels, but nor did everyone who partook of the fighting in Paris, Milan and Vienna earlier in the year. Usually, only a small cohort of genuine revolutionaries attempted to shape events as they unfolded. In Ballingarry, William Smith O'Brien, Terence Bellew MacManus, James Stephens and John Kavanagh, at least, were clearly engaged in an act of overt rebellion. Their success and circumstances differed greatly from the rebels of Sicily or France but their intentions were the same.

Ballingarry was a failure, but so too were most of the revolutions across Europe, the delirium of the 'springtime of the peoples' giving way to the despair of the counter-revolution and the return of the conservative old order. Alexander Herzen, the Russian exile, had a dream in later years about 1848 in which he was 'carried away again by the events that seethed around me' when all Europe 'took up its bed and walked – in a fit of somnambulism which we took for awakening'. The 'awakening' had proved false and Herzen's hopes had been dashed. Yet he did not envy 'those who were not carried away by that exquisite dream'.[2] The Young Irelanders, at least, had dreamed.

Appendix 1

Subscriptions from Limerick to the Irish Confederation

Place	Date	No. of Subscribers	Amount
Limerick	20 Feb. 1847	1	£1 0s 0d
Limerick	22 Feb. 1847	1	£3 0s 0d
Limerick	23 Feb. 1847	1	£1 0s 0d
Newcastle West	25 Feb. 1847	1	£0 1s 0d
Rathkeale	3 Mar. 1847	1	£0 2s 0d
Limerick	4 Mar. 1847	5	£1 0s 0d
Rathkeale	6 Apr. 1847	1	£0 1s 0d
Newcastle West	22 May 1847	5	£1 13s 2d
Newcastle West	12 July 1847	1	£0 1s 0d
Limerick	4 Aug. 1847	1	£0 2s 6d
Rathkeale	6 Aug. 1847	11	£9 0s 0d
Limerick	7 Sept. 1847	1	£0 5s 0d
Limerick	13 Sept. 1847	82	£16 0s 0d
Limerick	3 Oct. 1847	34	£3 10s 0d
Limerick	19 Oct. 1847	10	£3 10s 0d
Limerick	9 Nov. 1847	33	£3 19s 12d
Limerick	31 Dec. 1847	18	£1 17s 0d
Limerick	9 Jan. 1848	1	£2 0s 0d
Limerick	17 Feb. 1848	1	£1 0s 0d
Newcastle West	17 Apr. 1848	1	£1 0s 0d
Limerick	19 Apr. 1848	2	£4 0s 0d
Rathkeale	1 May 1848	4	£2 2s 0d
Limerick	1 May 1848	2	£0 12s 6d
Limerick	16 May 1848	1	£0 1s 0d
Rathkeale	19 May 1848	38	£12 9s 0d
Athea	9 June 1848	1	£1 0s 0d

Source: RIA, 23/H/62, subscription book of the Irish Confederation, 1847–48

Appendix 2

The Limerick Clubs

Name	President/Officers	Membership
Sarsfield Club, Limerick	William Smith O'Brien/ John O'Donnell	400–500
Felon Club, Newcastle West	William Fuller Hartnett	200–300
Brian Boru Club, Rathkeale	Patrick O'Dea	300–400
Hugh O'Neill Club, Limerick	James McCarthy	100
John Mitchel Club, Limerick	John McClenahan	100
Treaty Stone Club, Limerick	Patrick McNamara	100
Brian Boru Club, Limerick	R.W. Healy	100
Oliver Bond Club, Abbeyfeale	Charles Hughes	50
Kilmallock United Repealers' Club		50
Frank Arthur Club, Limerick		50
St John's Club, Limerick		50
Garryowen Club, Limerick		50

Mercantile Assistants' Club, Limerick		50
John Mitchel Club, Newcastle West	Daniel Moore	50
Bruff		50
Castle Mahon		50
Knockaderry		50
Ardagh		50

Sources: *Nation, Limerick Reporter, Limerick Chronicle* and RIA, 23/H/43, list of confederate clubs in Munster

APPENDIX 3

LIMERICK MEMBERS OF THE COUNCIL OF THE IRISH CONFEDERATION (1848)

William Smith O'Brien, landlord, Cahirmoyle
W.H. de Massy, landlord, Glenwilliam Castle
Revd Dr O'Connor, Limerick
John O'Donnell, solicitor, Limerick
John Dowling, solicitor, Newcastle West
James Kenny, doctor, Newcastle West
Daniel Griffin, doctor, Limerick
Alderman Charles O'Hara, merchant, Limerick
Alderman Michael Dawson, merchant, Limerick

Source: *Nation*

NOTES

List of Abbreviations

CCCA   Cork City and County Archives
LCA   Limerick City Archives
LCM   Limerick City Museum
NAI   National Archives of Ireland
NLI   National Library of Ireland
RIA   Royal Irish Academy
TCD   Trinity College, Dublin

Introduction

1   Osborne, C., *Verdi: A Life in the Theatre* (Weidenfeld & Nicolson, London, 1987), p. 88; Samson, J., *Chopin* (Oxford University Press, Oxford, 1998), p. 258; Walker, A., *Franz Liszt: The Weimar Years, 1848–1861* (Cornell University Press, New York, 1989), p. 71; Berthold, D., 'Melville, Garibaldi and the Medusa of Revolution', *American Literary History*, no. 9 (1997), p. 425.

2   O'Flaherty, L., *Famine* (Wolfhound Press, Dublin, 1994), pp. 385–6.

3   Owens, G., 'Popular mobilisation and the rising of 1848: the clubs of the Irish Confederation' in Geary, L. (ed.), *Rebellion and Remembrance in Modern Ireland* (Four Courts Press, Dublin, 2001), pp. 51–2.

Chapter 1: 'Secession'

1   Peter, A., *Dublin Fragments: Social and Historic* (Hodges, Figgis & Co., Dublin, 1925), pp. 163–4; MacDonagh, O., *O'Connell: The Life of Daniel O'Connell 1775–1847* (Weidenfeld & Nicolson, London, 1991), p. 513.

2   *Freeman's Journal*, 29 July 1846.

3   NLI, O'Brien papers, 437/1660, Ray to O'Brien, 11 July 1846 (emphasis in original).

4   *Nation*, 22 Nov. 1845; Quinn, J., *John Mitchel* (University College Dublin Press, Dublin, 2008), p. 11.

5   *Freeman's Journal*, 14 July 1846.

6   *Ibid.*, 29 July 1846.

7   *Ibid.*

8   *Ibid.*, 12 June 1846.

9   Davis, R. and Davis, M. (eds), *The Rebel in his Family: Selected Papers of William Smith O'Brien* (Cork University Press, Cork, 1998), pp. 47-8.

10 *Freeman's Journal*, 29 July 1846.

11 Mitchel, J., *Memoir of Thomas Devin Reilly* (P.M. Haverty, New York, 1857), p. 14; O'Leary, J., *Recollections of Fenians and Fenianism*, 2 vols (Irish University Press, Shannon, 1969), vol. 1, p. 14; Phelan, J., *The Ardent Exile: The Life and Times of Thomas D'Arcy McGee* (Macmillan, Toronto, 1951), p. 116.

12 Quinn, *Mitchel*, p. 9; Ó Cathaoir, B., 'Dillon, John Blake (1814-1866)', *Oxford Dictionary of National Biography* (Oxford University Press, Oxford, 2004); McGee, J.E., *The Men of '48* (Irish National Publishing House, Boston, 1881), p. 244.

13 *Nation*, 1 Aug. 1846; Davis, R., *The Young Ireland Movement* (Gill & Macmillan, Dublin, 1987), p. 103; NLI, O'Brien papers, 454, Rough Diary, 28 July 1846.

Chapter 2: 'The murderers of O'Connell'

1   *Limerick Reporter*, 23 Feb. 1847; *Limerick and Clare Examiner*, 24 Feb. 1847.

2   O'Neill Daunt, W.J., *Personal Recollections of the Late Daniel O'Connell*, 2 vols (Chapman & Hall, London, 1848), vol. 2, pp. 255-6.

3   *Hansard* (House of Commons), 8 Feb. 1847, vol. 89, col. 944.

4   *Limerick Reporter*, 28 May, 1 June 1847.

5   Sperber, J., *The European Revolutions, 1848-1851* (Cambridge University Press, Cambridge, 1995), p. 105.

6   Ó Grada, C., *Black '47 and Beyond: The Great Irish Famine in History, Economy and Memory* (Princeton University Press, Princeton, 1999), p. 203; *Limerick Reporter*, 26 March 1847.

7   NAI, outrage reports, 17/110, 22 Jan. 1847; *Limerick Reporter*, 1 June 1847.

8   Hannan, K., 'The Famine in Limerick', *Old Limerick Journal* (1995), p. 21; *Limerick Reporter*, 25 May 1847; Thackeray, W.M., *The Irish Sketchbook of 1842* (Nonsuch, Dublin, 2005), pp. 132-3.

9   Flaubert, G., *Sentimental Education* (Wordsworth Editions, Hertfordshire, 2003), p. 18; Namier, L., *1848: The Revolution of the Intellectuals* (Geoffrey Cumberlege, London, 1944), p. 3.

10 *Limerick Reporter*, 15 Jan., 9 March 1847.

11 *Limerick Reporter*, 29 Jan. 1847; CCCA, Denny Lane papers, U611/21, Duffy to Lane, 19 Dec. 1846.

12 *Pilot*, 15 Jan. 1847; MacDonagh, *O'Connell*, p. 593.

13 *Limerick Reporter*, 6 Aug. 1847.

14 RIA, 23/H/44, minute book of the Council of the Confederation, 26, 31 May 1847.

15 *Ibid.*, 4 June 1847; *Limerick Reporter*, 6 Aug. 1847.

16 *Limerick Reporter*, 6 Aug. 1847.

17 *Ibid.*, 10 Aug. 1847; NLI, O'Brien papers, 439/1961, Pigot to O'Brien, 15 Aug. 1847; NLI, O'Brien papers, 439/1996, O'Donnell to O'Brien, 19 Sept. 1847.

18 *Limerick Reporter*, 27 & 30 July 1847; NLI, O'Brien papers, 439/1946, O'Grady to O'Brien, 2 Aug. 1847.

19 *Limerick Reporter*, 6 Aug. 1847.

20 *Citizen*, 20 Oct., 22 Dec. 1855.

21 *Limerick Reporter*, 10 Aug. 1847; Hoppen, K.T., *Elections, Politics and Society in Ireland: 1832–1885* (Clarendon Press, Oxford, 1984), pp. 400–1.

22 *Limerick Reporter*, 10 & 13 Aug. 1848.

23 NLI, O'Brien papers, 439/1951, Fitzgerald to O'Brien, 5 Aug. 1847; NLI, O'Brien papers, 439/1958, Griffin to O'Brien, 9 Aug. 1847; Davis, *Young Ireland*, p. 91.

24 *Limerick Reporter*, 17 Aug. 1847.

25 *Ibid.*, 15 June 1847; NLI, O'Brien papers, 437/1670, O'Donnell to O'Brien, 4 Aug. 1846; NLI, O'Brien papers, 439/1944, O'Donnell to O'Brien, 1 Aug. 1847; NLI, O'Brien papers, 439/1976, Doyle to O'Brien, 3 Sept. 1847.

26 *Limerick Reporter*, 17 Aug., 3 Sept. 1847; NLI, O'Brien papers, 439/1967, Dowling to O'Brien, 19 Aug. 1847.

27 *Limerick Reporter*, 3 Sept. 1847.

28 *Nation*, 21 Aug. 1847.

29 NLI, O'Brien papers, 441/2263, Duffy memorandum, undated.

30 *Limerick Reporter*, 20 July 1847.

31 NLI, O'Brien papers, 439/1979, McClenahan to O'Brien, 4 Sept. 1847.

32 *Ibid.*, 439/1988, McClenahan to O'Brien, 11 Sept. 1847.

33 *Limerick Reporter*, 14 Sept. 1847.

34 NLI, O'Brien papers, 439/1995, Doyle to O'Brien, 18 Sept. 1847; RIA, 23/H/62, subscription book, 13 Sept., 3 Oct. 1847.

35 NLI, O'Brien papers, 441/2256, Duffy to O'Brien, undated; *Limerick Reporter*, 17 & 21 Sept., 8 Oct. 1847.

36 *Limerick Reporter*, 20 Aug. 1847; NLI, O'Brien papers, 441/2267, O'Gorman to O'Brien, 24 Dec. 1847.

37 Rapport, M., *1848: Year of Revolution* (Little, Brown, London, 2008), p. 39.

38 NLI, O'Brien papers, 439/1983, Mitchel to O'Brien, 8 Sept. 1847;

NLI, O'Brien papers, 439/2000, O'Donnell to O'Brien, 29 Sept. 1847.

39　*Ibid.*, 441/2281, O'Gorman to O'Brien, 1847.

40　*Limerick Reporter*, 19 & 22 Oct. 1847.

41　*Ibid.*, 22 & 26 Oct. 1847; NLI, O'Brien papers, 439/2026, Griffin to O'Brien, 1 Dec. 1847.

42　*Limerick Reporter*, 17 & 28 Sept. 1847.

43　*Ibid.*, 28 Sept., 15 Oct., 19 Nov. 1847.

44　*Hansard* (House of Commons), 29 Nov. 1847, vol. 95, cols 272–7; NAI, outrage reports, 17/1881, 13 Nov. 1847; *Limerick Reporter*, 14 Dec. 1847.

45　RIA, 12/P/15/7, Lalor to Mitchel, 21 June 1847; NLI, O'Brien papers, 439/1956, Mitchel to O'Brien, 8 Aug. 1847.

46　Quinn, *Mitchel*, pp. 22–3; RIA, 12/P/15/7, Lalor to Mitchel, 21 June 1847.

47　*Limerick Reporter*, 24 Dec. 1847.

Chapter 3: 'Times of storm and unrest'

1　Sloan, R., *William Smith O'Brien and the Young Ireland Rebellion of 1848* (Four Courts Press, Dublin, 2000), p. 195.

2　NLI, O'Brien papers, MS 441/2235, Duffy to O'Brien, 11 Dec. 1847.

3　*Limerick Reporter*, 14 Jan. 1848.

4　*Nation*, 8 Jan. 1848; *Limerick Reporter*, 14 Jan. 1848.

5　*Limerick Reporter*, 14 Jan. 1848.

6　*Limerick Chronicle*, 12 Jan. 1848.

7　Mitchel, J., *Jail Journal* (Burns, Oates & Washbourne, London, n.d.), p. 17.

8　*Limerick Reporter*, 1 Feb. 1848.

9　NLI, O'Brien papers, 441/2355, O'Gorman to O'Brien, 18 Jan. 1848.

10　Sloan, *O'Brien*, pp. 207–8.

11　*Limerick Chronicle*, 26 Feb. 1848; Sloan, *O'Brien*, p. 209.

12　Flaubert, *Sentimental Education*, pp. 303–4.

13　*Limerick Reporter*, 29 Feb., 7 March 1848.

14　*Ibid.*, 7 & 14 March 1848.

15　*Ibid.*, 29 Feb. 1848; NAI, outrage reports, 17/257, 3 March 1848; 17/253, 5 March 1848.

16　Ó Murchadha, C., 'Limerick Union workhouse during the Great Famine', *Old Limerick Journal* (1995), p. 42; *Nation*, 15 April 1848.

17　Cronin, M., 'Young Ireland in Cork, 1840–49' in Dunne. T. and Geary. L. (eds), *History and the Public Sphere: Essays in Honour of*

John A. Murphy (Cork University Press, Cork, 2005), p. 121; Sloan, *O'Brien*, p. 211.

18 Legg, M.-L. (ed.), *Alfred Webb: The Autobiography of a Quaker Nationalist* (Cork University Press, Cork, 1999), pp. 17–18; O'Leary, *Fenians and Fenianism*, pp. 7–8.

19 NLI, O'Brien papers, 442/2383, O'Gorman to O'Brien, 4 March 1848; NLI, O'Brien papers, 441/2255, Duffy to O'Brien, undated 1848; Sloan, *O'Brien*, p. 210; Duffy, C.G., *Four Years of Irish History, 1845–1849* (Cassell, Petter, Galpin & Co., London, 1883), pp. 548–50.

20 Mitchel, *Jail Journal*, p. 17; Sloan, *O'Brien*, p. 212; NLI, O'Brien papers, 441/2344, Duffy to O'Brien, 1848 (no precise date).

21 *Limerick Reporter*, 7 March 1848; NLI, O'Brien papers, 442/2390, O'Donnell to O'Brien, 9 March 1848.

22 *Limerick Reporter*, 21 March 1848.

23 Mann, T., *Buddenbrooks* (Vintage, London, 1999), p. 153.

24 *Nation*, 18 March 1848; Rapport, *1848*, p. 76.

25 *Limerick Reporter*, 14 & 17 March 1848.

26 NLI, O'Brien papers, 442/2397, Pigot to O'Brien, 16 March 1848.

27 *Limerick Reporter*, 17 & 21 March 1848.

28 NAI, outrage reports, 17/327, 22 March 1848.

29 *Limerick Reporter*, 28 March 1848; *Limerick Chronicle*, 29 March 1848.

30 *Limerick Reporter*, 28 March 1848.

31 *Ibid.*

32 *Nation*, 18 March 1848.

33 *Limerick Reporter*, 24 March 1848.

34 NAI, outrage reports, 17/376, 2 April 1848; *Limerick Chronicle*, 29 May 1847.

35 NAI, outrage reports, 17/376, 2 April 1848; Ó Murchadha, 'Limerick Union workhouse', p. 42.

36 *Nation*, 22 April 1848; NAI, outrage reports, 17/374, 3 April 1848; NLI, O'Brien papers, 17/418, 8 April 1848; Owens, 'Popular Mobilisation', pp. 60–1; *Limerick Reporter*, 25 April 1848.

37 *Limerick Reporter*, 31 March, 4 April 1848; *Nation*, 22 April 1848.

38 *Limerick Reporter*, 14 April 1848; Mitchel, *Jail Journal*, p. 18.

39 *Limerick Reporter*, 14 April 1848.

40 NAI, outrage reports, 17/555, 17 April 1848; 17/583, 21 April 1848.

41 *Ibid.*, 17/573, 20 April 1848.

42 *Limerick Chronicle*, 29 March 1848. The Clonmel magistrate, William Ryan, also mentions this incident in a report, stating 'the district of

Kilsheelan was illuminated with fires and they also extended into the county of Waterford in consequence of a report that reached Carrick-on-Suir that His Excellency [Clarendon] had left Dublin through fear'. Nolan, W., 'The Irish Confederation in County Tipperary in 1848', *Tipperary Historical Journal* (1998), p. 6.

43   *Limerick Reporter*, 4 & 7 April 1848.
44   NAI, outrage reports, 17/596, 26 April 1848.

Chapter 4: The 'attack on the life of Mr Mitchel'

1   *Limerick Reporter*, 14 & 18 April 1848.
2   *Ibid.*, 25 April 1848; *Limerick Chronicle*, 26 April 1848.
3   *Limerick Reporter*, 28 April 1848.
4   *Ibid.*
5   *Ibid.*, 2 May 1848.
6   NLI, O'Brien papers, 441/2255, Duffy to O'Brien, 1848 (no precise date).
7   LCM, 5126, minute book of Limerick Society for the Promotion of Literary, Scientific and Industrial Education, 1847–49, p. 5; *Limerick Reporter*, 14 April 1848.
8   *Limerick Chronicle*, 29 April 1848; Dillon, W., *Life of John Mitchel*, 2 vols (Kegan Paul, Trench & Co., London, 1888), vol. 1, p. 227.
9   *Limerick Reporter*, 28 April, 2 May 1848; *Limerick Chronicle*, 3 May 1848.
10   Gwynn, D., *Young Ireland and 1848* (Cork University Press, Cork, 1949), pp. 174–7.
11   *Limerick Reporter*, 2 May 1848; *Limerick Chronicle*, 3 May 1848.
12   Duffy, C.G., *Conversations with Carlyle* (Athol Books, Belfast, 2005), p. 137; *Limerick Reporter*, 2 May 1848; *Limerick Chronicle*, 3 May 1848.
13   *Limerick Reporter*, 2 May 1848; Sloan, *O'Brien*, p. 227.
14   *Limerick Reporter*, 2 May 1848.
15   *Limerick Chronicle*, 3 May 1848; *Limerick Reporter*, 5 May 1848.
16   *Limerick Reporter*, 9 May 1848; *Limerick Chronicle*, 3 May 1848.
17   *Limerick Reporter*, 12 May 1848; Lysaght, P., 'Bartholomew Dowling', *Old Limerick Journal* (1996), p. 13; LCM, 5126, minute book of Limerick Society for the Promotion of Literary, Scientific and Industrial Education, 1847–49, p. 15.
18   *Limerick Reporter*, 2 & 5 May 1848.
19   *Freeman's Journal*, 2, 4 & 6 May 1848.
20   *Nation*, 6 May 1848; Duffy, C.G., *My Life in Two Hemispheres*, 2 vols (Irish University Press, Shannon, 1969), vol. 1, p. 271.
21   *United Irishman*, 6 May 1848; Gwynn, *Young Ireland and 1848*,

    p. 178.

22   *World*, 6 May 1848.

23   Mitchel, *Jail Journal*, p. 17; Legg, M.-L. (ed.), *Newspapers and Nationalism: The Irish Provincial Press, 1850–1892* (Four Courts Press, Dublin, 1999), pp. 64–5.

24   *The Times*, 3 & 4 May 1848.

25   NLI, O'Brien papers, 442/2428, Guild of Carpenters to O'Brien, 30 April 1848; *Freeman's Journal*, 6 May 1848; Davis, *The Young Ireland Movement*, p. 153.

26   *Nation*, 6 May 1848; *Limerick Chronicle*, 3 May 1848.

Chapter 5: 'Prepare, ye Men of '48'

  1   *Hansard* (House of Lords), 10 April 1848, vol. 98, col. 71; Storey, G. and Fielding, K.J. (eds), *The Letters of Charles Dickens: 1847–1849* (Clarendon Press, Oxford, 1981), p. 273.

  2   Sigmann, J., *1848: The Romantic and Democratic Revolutions in Europe* (George Allen & Unwin, London, 1973), p. 236; Kinealy, C., '"Brethren in Bondage": Chartists, O'Connellites, Young Irelanders and the 1848 uprising' in Lane, F. and Ó Drisceoil, D. (eds), *Politics and the Irish Working Class, 1830–1945* (Palgrave Macmillan, Basingstoke, 2005), p. 100.

  3   Young, G.M., *Victorian England: Portrait of an Age* (Oxford University Press, London, 1961), p. 78; Wilson, A.N., *The Victorians* (Arrow Books, London, 2003), p. 117.

  4   Kinealy, 'Brethren in bondage', p. 101; Belchem, J., 'The Waterloo of peace and order: the United Kingdom and the revolutions of 1848' in Dowe, D. *et al.* (eds), *Europe in 1848: Revolution and Reform* (Berghahn Books, New York and Oxford, 2001), p. 250; Huggins, M., '"Mere matters of arrangement and detail": John Mitchel and Irish Chartism' in Swift, R. and Kinealy, C. (eds), *Politics and Power in Victorian Ireland* (Four Courts Press, Dublin, 2006), p. 104.

  5   *Hansard* (House of Commons), 10 April 1848, vol. 98, cols 74–7.

  6   The Treason Felony Act was a tactically astute piece of legislation carrying a maximum penalty of transportation for life. It created for the government a middle path of prosecution between the mandatory death sentence for high treason and the relatively minor penalties that accompanied charges of sedition. The Act remains in force today despite a legal challenge by the republican *Guardian* newspaper in 2001. See the *Guardian*, 26 June 2003.

  7   NLI, O'Brien papers, 442/2417, O'Dea to O'Brien, 19 April 1848.

  8   Rapport, *1848*, p. 190.

  9   *Limerick Reporter*, 19 May 1848; *Limerick Chronicle*, 20 & 24 May

1848; *The Times*, 29 May 1848.

10   *Limerick Reporter*, 26 & 30 May 1848.

11   *Limerick Chronicle*, 31 May 1848; Cronin, 'Young Ireland in Cork', p. 121; Mitchel, *Jail Journal*, p. 20.

12   Palmer, S., *Police and Protest in England and Ireland: 1780–1850* (Cambridge University Press, Cambridge, 1988), p. 483; NLI, Duffy papers, 5886, narrative by O'Gorman, pp. 11–12; TCD, police reports, 2038, 25 May 1848.

13   LCA, De Vere papers, P22/402/16, O'Brien to De Vere, 9 May 1848; Sloan, *O'Brien*, p. 232.

14   Mitchel, *Jail Journal*, p. 21; Owens, 'Popular mobilisation', pp. 55–6; TCD, police reports, 2038, 26 May 1848.

15   Duffy, *My Life*, vol. 1, p. 278.

16   Belchem, J., 'Republican spirit and military science: the "Irish Brigade" and Irish-American nationalism in 1848', *Irish Historical Studies*, vol. 29 (May 1994), pp. 46, 55.

17   *Limerick Reporter*, 9, 16 & 23 June, 4 July 1848; Mitchel, *Jail Journal*, p. 36.

18   *Limerick Chronicle*, 1 July 1848; Davis, R. *Revolutionary Imperialist: William Smith O'Brien, 1803–1864* (Lilliput Press, Dublin, 1998), p. 258.

19   Rapport, *1848*, p. 208.

20   MacDonagh, *O'Connell*, p. 597; Rapport, *1848*, pp. 206–7; *Limerick Chronicle*, 17 May, 10 June, 15 July 1848.

21   *Limerick Reporter*, 4 July 1848.

22   NLI, O'Brien papers, 442/2482, O'Donnell to O'Brien, 25 June 1848.

23   *Limerick Reporter*, 20 & 23 June, 11 July 1848; *Nation*, 15 July 1848.

24   NAI, outrage reports, 17/939, 6 July 1848; 17/946, 7 July 1848.

25   *Ibid.*, 17/944, 8 July 1848; RIA, 23/H/63, income book of Irish Confederation, 24 June 1848; Belchem, 'Republican spirit and military science', pp. 60–3.

26   NAI, outrage reports, 17/971, 14 July 1848; *Limerick Reporter*, 18 July 1848.

27   NAI, outrage reports, 17/982, 15 July 1848; *ibid.*, 17/1099, 29 July 1848.

28   *Limerick Reporter*, 18 July 1848.

29   NAI, outrage reports, 17/944, 8 July 1848; Owens, 'Popular mobilisation', p. 62.

30   NAI, outrage reports, 17/982, 15 July 184; *Limerick Reporter*, 18 July 1848; Doheny, M., *The Felon's Track* (M.H. Gill & Son, Dublin,

1918), p. 155.

31   *Limerick Reporter*, 21 July 1848.

32   TCD, police reports, 2038, 18 April 1848; *Limerick Reporter*, 18 July 1848.

33   CCCA, Denny Lane papers, U611/47, 16 June 1848.

34   *Ibid.*, U611/48, O'Gorman to Lane, 8 July 1848.

35   NLI, Duffy papers, 5886, narrative of O'Gorman, pp. 13–14.

36   *Ibid.*, p. 14; *Limerick Reporter*, 25 July 1848; *Limerick Chronicle*, 26 July 1848.

37   NAI, outrage reports, 17/1012, 23 July 1848; *Limerick Reporter*, 25 July 1848.

38   *Limerick Chronicle*, 26 July 1848; *Limerick and Clare Examiner*, 26 July 1848; NAI, outrage reports, 17/1039, 26 July 1848.

39   *Limerick Reporter*, 25 July 1848; *Limerick Chronicle*, 26 July 1848.

40   NAI, outrage reports, 17/1162, 31 July 1848.

41   *Ibid.*, 17/1053, 30 July 1848; 17/1100, 2 Aug. 1848.

42   *Ibid.*, 17/1048, 30 July 1848.

43   *Ibid.*

44   *Ibid.*, 17/1458, 28 July 1848; *Limerick Chronicle*, 5, 12, 22 & 26 July 1848; *Limerick Reporter*, 25 July 1848.

Chapter 6: Insurrection at Abbeyfeale

1   Lewis, S., *A History and Topography of Limerick City and County* (Mercier Press, Cork, 1980), p. 36; NAI, outrage reports, 17/1064, 31 July 1848.

2   The best accounts of events in Ballingarry are in Davis, *Revolutionary Imperialist*, pp. 271–6 and Sloan, *O'Brien*, pp. 275–81.

3   Sloan, *O'Brien*, p. 279.

4   *Limerick Reporter*, 4 Aug. 1848.

5   Kinealy, C., *Repeal and Revolution: 1848 in Ireland* (Manchester University Press, Manchester, 2009), p. 199; *Cork Examiner*, 31 July, 2 Aug. 1848.

6   Ó Cathaoir, B., *Young Irelander Abroad: The Diary of Charles Hart* (Cork University Press, Cork, 2003), p. 33; Sloan, *O'Brien*, p. 273.

7   *Cork Examiner*, 6 Aug. 1848.

8   *Ibid.*, 11 & 16 Aug. 1848.

9   Sloan, *O'Brien*, pp. 249–53.

10   Nolan, 'The Irish Confederation in County Tipperary', pp. 4–11; Doheny, *Felon's Track*, pp. 162–4.

11   Doheny, *Felon's Track*, p. 168.

12   TCD, police reports, 2038, 18 July 1848.

13   Owens, 'Patrick O'Donohoe's narrative of the 1848 rising', *Tipperary*

Historical Journal (1998), pp. 34-6.

14   Kinealy, *Repeal and Revolution*, p. 196; McAllister, T.G., *Terence Bellew McManus: 1811(?)-1861* (St Patrick's College, Maynooth, 1972), p. 10; CCCA, Denny Lane papers, U611/46, MacManus to Lane, 9 Feb. 1848; Sloan, *O'Brien*, pp. 267, 274.

15   LCA, De Vere papers, P22/394/68-70, O'Brien to De Vere, 20 July 1848.

16   NLI, Duffy papers, 5886, narrative of O'Gorman, p. 15.

17   *Cork Examiner*, 4 Aug. 1848.

18   NLI, Duffy papers, 5886, narrative of O'Gorman, pp. 15–16.

19   *Limerick Reporter*, 1 Aug. 1848.

20   *Ibid.*; NLI, Duffy papers, 5886, narrative of O'Gorman, p. 16.

21   *Limerick Chronicle*, 9 Aug. 1848.

22   NAI, outrage reports, 17/1253, 3 Aug. 1848; 17/1869/encl 2, 5 Aug. 1848; *Kerry Evening Post*, 5 Aug. 1848.

23   NAI, outrage reports, 17/1253, 3 Aug. 1848; 17/1869/encl 2, 5 Aug. 1848.

24   Freeman, T.W., 'Land and People, *c.* 1841' in Vaughan, W.E. (ed.), *A New History of Ireland: Ireland Under the Union, 1801-70* (Clarendon Press, Oxford, 1989), p. 256; *Kerry Evening Post*, 5 Aug. 1848; *Limerick Chronicle*, 12 Aug. 1848; *Limerick Reporter*, 15 Aug. 1848.

25   NAI, outrage reports, 17/1869/encl 1, 6 Aug. 1848; 17/1108, 5 Aug. 1848; *Kerry Evening Post*, 5 Aug. 1848.

26   NAI, outrage reports, 17/1869/encl 2, 5 Aug. 1848.

27   LCM, 2004.0053, *New York Daily Tribune*, 28 Aug. 1848; NAI, outrage reports, 17/1112, 7 Aug. 1848; *Limerick Chronicle*, 12 Aug. 1848.

28   NAI, outrage reports, 17/1108, 5 Aug. 1848; 17/1869/encl 2, 5 Aug. 1848; Duffy, *Four Years*, p. 678.

29   NLI, Duffy papers, 5886, narrative of O'Gorman, p. 18; Miller, K., *Emigrants and Exiles* (Oxford University Press, Oxford, 1988), p. 309.

Chapter 7: 'On the run'

1   Nolan, W., 'The final days of Meagher's Irish uprising' in Hearne, J.M. and Cornish, R.T. (eds), *Thomas Francis Meagher: The Making of an Irish American* (Irish Academic Press, Dublin, 2006), p. 96.

2   *Limerick Reporter*, 17 Oct. 1848; *Limerick Chronicle*, 1 Nov. 1848; Nolan, 'Meagher's Irish uprising', p. 103.

3   *Cork Examiner*, 16 Aug. 1848.

4   *Limerick Chronicle*, 9 Aug. 1848; *Cork Examiner*, 9 Aug. 1848.

5   *Limerick Chronicle*, 9 & 26 Aug. 1848; *Limerick and Clare Examiner*,

9 Aug. 1848.

6   NAI, outrage reports, 17/1272, 18 Aug. 1848; 17/1186, 18 Aug. 1848.

7   *Limerick Reporter*, 5 Sept. 1848.

8   *Ibid.*, 15 & 25 Aug. 1848; *Cork Examiner*, 30 Aug. 1848.

9   NAI, outrage reports, 17/1134, 9 Aug. 1848; *Limerick Chronicle*, 5, 12 July 1848; *Limerick Reporter*, 18 June, 10 Sept. 1847.

10 NAI, outrage reports, 17/1164, 14 Aug. 1848; 17/1180, 16 Aug. 1848; 17/1588, 24 Oct. 1848; 17/1201, 20 Aug. 1848; 17/1300, 31 Aug. 1848.

11 Duffy, *Four Years*, p. 677; *Limerick Reporter*, 12 Dec. 1848.

12 NAI, outrage reports, 17/1506, 9 Oct. 1848; 17/1695, 18 Nov. 1848.

13 *Cork Examiner*, 6 & 14 Aug. 1848; *Limerick Reporter*, 11 Aug. 1848.

14 *Limerick Reporter*, 4 Aug., 10 Nov. 1848.

15 *Citizen*, 20 Oct. 1855; *Limerick Reporter*, 8 & 18 Aug. 1848; *Limerick Chronicle*, 16 Aug. 1848; *Cork Examiner*, 30 Aug. 1848.

16 *Limerick Chronicle*, 26 Aug. 1848.

17 *Limerick and Clare Examiner*, 2 Aug. 1848.

18 Duffy, *Four Years*, p. 769; TCD, police reports, 2038, 9 Aug. 1848; *Limerick and Clare Examiner*, 12 Aug. 1848; *Cork Examiner*, 30 Aug. 1848.

19 *Limerick Chronicle*, 26 Aug. 1848; Doheny, *Felon's Track*, p. 283; Davis, *Young Ireland*, p. 165; Kinealy, *Repeal and Revolution*, p. 202.

20 *The Sunday Times* is quoted in *Limerick Reporter*, 25 Aug., 12 Sept., 13 Oct. 1848; *The Times*, 25 Aug. 1848.

21 NLI, Duffy papers, 5886, narrative of O'Gorman, p. 1.

22 *Ibid.*, p. 16; Ó Conchubhair, P., '"Not so much about the cabbage garden!": Kerry and the year of revolution – 1848', *The Kerry Magazine* (1998), p. 47.

23 NAI, outrage reports, 17/1203, 13 Aug. 1848.

24 *Ibid.*, 17/1418, 29 Aug. 1848.

25 NAI, outrage reports, 17/1429, 26 Sept. 1848; *Limerick Chronicle*, 27 Sept. 1848.

26 *Limerick Reporter*, 15 Aug. 1848; *Limerick Chronicle*, 19 Aug. 1848.

27 NLI, Duffy papers, 5886, narrative of O'Gorman, pp. 17–18.

28 *Munster News*, 22 Nov. 1865; Murphy, I., *Father Michael Meehan and the Ark of Kilbaha* (Cross, Ennis, 1980), pp. 1–5.

29 *Limerick Reporter*, 19 Sept. 1848.

30 *Cork Examiner*, 16 Aug. 1848; NAI, outrage reports, 17/1397, 23 Sept. 1848.

31 NAI, outrage reports, 17/1418, 23 Sept. 1848.

32 *Ibid.*, 17/1399, 24 Sept. 1848; 17/1418, 25 Sept. 1848; 17/1429, 26 Sept. 1848.
33 *Ibid.*, 17/1364, 17 Sept. 1848.
34 *Limerick Reporter*, 22 & 26 Sept., 1 & 22 Dec. 1848.

Chapter 8: 'The exile's lot'
1   Sloan, *O'Brien*, p. 297; CCCA, Denny Lane papers, U611/54, Martin to Lane, 17 June 1849.
2   Davis, 'From Limerick to Van Diemen's Land: Irish transportation at work', *Old Limerick Journal* (1999), pp. 34–8.
3   *Nation*, 3 & 10 June 1848.
4   *Irish American*, 19 June 1852.
5   Keneally, T., *The Great Shame: A Story of the Irish in the Old World and the New* (Vintage, London, 1999), p. 280; Emmons, D., 'The strange death of Thomas Francis Meagher: tribal politics in territorial Montana' in Hearne and Cornish, *Meagher*, pp. 223–39.
6   Davis, 'Patrick O'Donohoe: outcast of the exiles' in Reece, B. (ed.), *Exiles from Erin: Convict Lives in Ireland and Australia* (Gill & Macmillan, Dublin, 1991), p. 269.
7   Quinn, *Mitchel*, p. 66.
8   Davis and Davis, *The Rebel in his Family*, p. 70.
9   University of Southampton, Broadlands (Palmerston) papers, GC/OB/2, Lady O'Brien to Palmerston, 15 May 1856; *Limerick Reporter & Tipperary Vindicator*, 24, & 28 June 1864.
10 Ó Cathaoir, *Young Irelander Abroad*, p. 39; Ó Cathaoir, B., *John Blake Dillon: Young Irelander* (Irish Academic Press, Dublin, 1990), p. 100.
11 Ó Cathaoir, *Young Irelander Abroad*, p. 42.
12 *Ibid.*, p. 43; O'Flaherty, P., 'Michael Doheny: Young Irelander and Fenian', *The Irish Sword* (1987–88), pp. 81–9.
13 Ó Cathaoir, *Dillon*, p. 129.
14 Duffy, *Four Years*, pp. 769–70; Savage, J., *'98 and '48: The Modern Revolutionary History and Literature of Ireland* (P.J. Kennedy, New York, 1882), p. 347.
15 NLI, O'Brien papers, 443/2532, O'Gorman to O'Brien, 16 Jan. 1849.
16 *Ibid.*, 443/2547, O'Gorman to O'Brien, 24 May 1849.
17 *Irish American*, 18 Sept. 1852.
18 Miller, K.A., *Ireland and Irish America: Culture, Class and Transatlantic Migration* (Field Day, Dublin, 2008), p. 288; O'Leary, *Fenians and Fenianism*, vol. 1, p. 95; NLI, Michael J. Lennon papers, 22,337/D/18, p. 10.

19   NLI, O'Brien papers, 445/2958, O'Gorman to O'Brien, 17 May
      1857; *The Times*, 1 Aug. 1859; *Nation*, 27 Aug. 1859.
20   NLI, O'Brien papers, 446/3082, O'Gorman to O'Brien, 1 Jan.
      1859.
21   *New York Times*, 2 March 1895.
22   NLI, Duffy papers, 5886, narrative by O'Gorman, pp. 20–2.
23   *Limerick Reporter*, 30 Jan., 27 Feb. 1849; *Citizen*, 7 Jan. 1854.
24   Lysaght, 'Dowling', p. 13.
25   *Limerick Reporter*, 9 & 12 Jan. 1849.
26   Ó Cathaoir, *Young Irelander Abroad*, pp. 42–3.
27   *Citizen*, 15 Dec. 1855; *New York Times*, 23 Feb., 18 May 1866.
28   *Limerick Reporter*, 22 Dec. 1848; *Limerick Chronicle*, 3 & 20 Oct.
      1849.
29   Duffy, *Four Years*, pp. 758–9; Doheny, *Felon's Track*, p. 305; *Irish
      American*, 27 Sept. 1856.
30   www.limerickcity.ie/Library/LocalStudies/GriffithsValuationofLim
      erickCity1850 (accessed 28 Sept. 2009).
31   LCM, 2004.0057, *Minutes of Evidence taken before the Select Committee
      on Limerick City Election Petition* (1859).
32   Ryan, D., *The Fenian Chief: A Biography of James Stephens* (M.H.
      Gill & Son, Dublin, 1967), p. 176; *Limerick Reporter & Tipperary
      Vindicator*, 28 June 1864; *Nation*, 28 Jan. 1865.
33   *Limerick Reporter & Tipperary Vindicator*, 19 Feb. 1869; *Nation*, 20
      Feb. 1869.
34   *Limerick Reporter & Tipperary Vindicator*, 1 July 1873; NLI, Duffy
      papers, 5886, narrative of O'Gorman, p. 15.

Chapter 9: 'This cursed Ballingarry'

1   Thackeray, *A Collection of Letters of W.M. Thackeray, 1847–1855*
      (Smith, Elder & Co, London, 1887), pp. 18–9.
2   *The Times*, 26, 27 & 28 July 1848; Dasent, A.I., *John Thadeus Delane:
      Editor. of 'The Times'*, 2 vols (John Murray, London, 1908), vol. 1,
      pp. 77–9.
3   *The Times*, 31 July, 1 & 2 Aug. 1848.
4   *Ibid.*, 2 Aug. 1848; *Nation* 9 April 1853; Davis, *Revolutionary
      Imperialist*, p. 357; Ó Broin, L., *Charles Gavan Duffy: Patriot and
      Statesman* (James Duffy & Co., Dublin, 1967), p. 115.
5   Quinn, *Mitchel*, p. 41; Mitchel, *Jail Journal*, p. 82.
6   Mitchel, *Jail Journal*, p. 84; Golway, T., *Irish Rebel: John Devoy and
      America's Fight for Irish Freedom* (St Martin's Griffin, New York,
      1999), p. 14.
7   Owens, 'O'Donohoe', p. 32.

8   Duffy, *Four Years*, p. 689.
9   Pearl, C., *The Three Lives of Gavan Duffy* (New South Wales University Press, New South Wales, 1979), p. 229; O'Donoghue, D.J., *Life and Writings of James Clarence Mangan* (M.H. Gill, Dublin, 1897); Collins, P., 'The contest of memory: the continuing impact of 1798 commemoration', *Éire-Ireland*, no. 34 (summer 1999), p. 38.
10   *Shan Van Vocht* Feb. 1898, p. 26; June 1898, p. 106.
11   Maume, P., 'Young Ireland, Arthur Griffith, and republican ideology: the question of continuity', *Éire-Ireland*, no. 34 (summer 1999), p. 161; Mitchell, A., *Casement* (Haus Publishing, London, 2003), p. 48; Kinealy, *Repeal and Revolution*, p. 259.
12   Maye, B., *Arthur Griffith* (Griffith College Publications, Dublin, 1997), p. 13; Maume, 'Young Ireland, Arthur Griffith, and republican ideology', p. 162.
13   *Studies*, Sept. 1919, p. 494; March 1918, p. 178; Quinn, *Mitchel*, p. 1.
14   Foster, R., *W.B. Yeats, a Life: I, the Apprentice Mage, 1865–1914* (Oxford University Press, Oxford and New York, 1998), p. 524; Collins, 'The contest of memory', pp. 45–6.
15   Edwards, R.D., 'The contribution of Young Ireland to the development of the Irish national idea' in Pendar, S. (ed.), *Essays and Studies Presented to Torna* (Cork University Press, Cork, 1947), p. 133; Lyons, F.S.L., *Ireland Since the Famine* (Weidenfeld & Nicolson, London, 1971), pp. 100–1; Ó Tuathaigh, G., *Ireland Before the Famine* (Gill & Macmillan, Dublin, 1979), pp. 201–2; Foster, R., *Modern Ireland: 1600–1972* (Allen Lane, London, 1988), p. 316; Donnolly, J.S., 'A famine in Irish politics' in Vaughan (ed.), *A New History of Ireland*, pp. 369–71.
16   Kinealy, *Repeal and Revolution*, p. 16; Huggins, 'Mitchel and Irish Chartism', p. 108.
17   Davis, *Young Ireland*, p. 264; *The Irish Times*, 31 July 1998.

Legacy

1   Palmer, *Police and Protest*, p. 501; Owens, 'O'Donohoe', p. 33.
2   Rapport, *1848*, p. 41

BIBLIOGRAPHY

Manuscript Sources
Cork City and County Archives
Denny Lane papers

Limerick City Archives
De Vere papers

Limerick City Museum
Minute book of Limerick Society for the Promotion of Literary, Scientific
and Industrial Education, 1847–49
Minutes of evidence taken before the Select Committee on Limerick City
Election Petition (1859)
New York Daily Tribune, 28 Aug. 1848

National Archives of Ireland
Outrage Reports, Limerick, 1847–48

National Library of Ireland
Charles Gavan Duffy papers
Michael J. Lennon papers
William Smith O'Brien papers

Royal Irish Academy
Correspondence book of Irish Confederation
Expenditure book of Irish Confederation
Minute book of Council of the Irish Confederation
Subscription book of Irish Confederation

Trinity College Dublin
Police reports

University of Southampton
Broadlands (Palmerston) Papers

Newspapers and Journals
Citizen
Clare Journal
Cork Examiner
Freeman's Journal
Guardian
Irish American

Irish Times
Kerry Evening Post
Limerick and Clare Examiner
Limerick Chronicle
Limerick Reporter
Limerick Reporter & Tipperary Vindicator
Munster News
Nation
New York Times
Pilot
Shan Van Vocht
Studies
The Times
United Irishman
World

Official Publications
Hansard Parliamentary Debates, third series, 1847–48

Internet
www.limerickcity.ie/Library/LocalStudies/GriffithsValuationofLim
    erickCity1850

Books and Articles
Belchem, J., 'Republican spirit and military science: The "Irish Brigade"
    and Irish-American nationalism in 1848', *Irish Historical Studies*,
    no. 29 (May 1994)
Belchem, J., 'The Waterloo of peace and order: The United Kingdom and
    the revolutions of 1848' in Dowe, D. *et al.* (eds), *Europe in 1848:
    Revolution and Reform* (Berghahn Books, New York and Oxford,
    2001)
Berthold, D., 'Melville, Garibaldi and the Medusa of Revolution', *American
    Literary History* 9 (1997)
Collins, P., 'The contest of memory: the continuing impact of 1798 com-
    memoration', *Éire-Ireland*, no. 34 (summer 1999)
Cronin, M., 'Young Ireland in Cork, 1840–49' in Dunne, T. and Geary,
    L. (eds), *History and the Public Sphere: Essays in Honour of John A.
    Murphy* (Cork University Press, Cork, 2005)
Dasent, A.I., *John Thadeus Delane: Editor of* The Times, 2 vols (John
    Murray, London, 1908)
Davis, R., *The Young Ireland Movement* (Gill & Macmillan, Dublin,
    1987)
Davis, R., 'Patrick O'Donohoe: outcast of the exiles' in Reece, B. (ed.),

Exiles from Erin: Convict Lives in Ireland and Australia (Gill & Macmillan, Dublin, 1991)

Davis, R., *Revolutionary Imperialist: William Smith O'Brien, 1803–1864* (Lilliput Press, Dublin, 1998)

Davis, R., 'From Limerick to Van Diemen's Land: Irish transportation at work', *Old Limerick Journal* (1999)

Davis, R. and Davis, M. (eds), *The Rebel in his Family: Selected Papers of William Smith O'Brien* (Cork University Press, Cork, 1998)

Dillon, W., *Life of John Mitchel*, 2 vols (Kegan Paul, Trench & Co., London, 1888)

Doheny, M., *The Felon's Track* (M.H. Gill & Son, Dublin, 1918)

Donnolly, J.S., 'A famine in Irish politics' in Vaughan, W.E. (ed.), *A New History of Ireland: Ireland Under the Union, 1801-70* (Clarendon Press, Oxford, 1989)

Duffy, C.G., *Four Years of Irish History, 1845–1849* (Cassell, Petter, Galpin & Co, London, 1883)

Duffy, C.G., *My Life in Two Hemispheres*, 2 vols (Irish University Press, Shannon, 1969)

Duffy, C.G., *Conversations with Carlyle* (Athol Books, Belfast, 2005)

Edwards, R.D., 'The contribution of Young Ireland to the development of the Irish national idea' in Pendar, S. (ed.), *Essays and Studies Presented to Torna* (Cork University Press, Cork, 1947)

Emmons, D., 'The strange death of Thomas Francis Meagher: tribal politics in territorial Montana' in Hearne, J.M. and Cornish, R.T. (eds), *Thomas Francis Meagher: The Making of an Irish American* (Irish Academic Press, Dublin, 2006)

Flaubert, G., *Sentimental Education* (Wordsworth Editions, Hertfordshire, 2003)

Foster, R., *Modern Ireland: 1600-1972* (Allen Lane, London, 1988)

Foster, R., *W.B. Yeats, a Life: I, the Apprentice Mage, 1865-1914* (Oxford University Press, Oxford and New York, 1998)

Freeman, T.W., 'Land and people, *c.* 1841' in Vaughan, W.E. (ed.), *A New History of Ireland: Ireland Under the Union, 1801-70* (Clarendon Press, Oxford, 1989)

Golway, T., *Irish Rebel: John Devoy and America's Fight for Irish Freedom* (St Martin's Griffin, New York, 1999)

Gwynn, D., *Young Ireland and 1848* (Cork University Press, Cork, 1949)

Hannan, K., 'The Famine in Limerick', *Old Limerick Journal* (1995)

Hoppen, K.T., *Elections, Politics and Society in Ireland: 1832-1885* (Clarendon Press, Oxford, 1984)

Huggins, M., '"Mere matters of arrangement and detail": John Mitchel and Irish Chartism' in Swift, R. and Kinealy, C. (eds), *Politics and Power in Victorian Ireland* (Four Courts Press, Dublin, 2006)

Keneally, T., *The Great Shame: A Story of the Irish in the Old World and the New* (Vintage, London, 1999)

Kinealy, C., '"Brethren in bondage": Chartists, O'Connellites, Young Irelanders and the 1848 uprising' in Lane, F. and Ó Drisceoil, D. (eds), *Politics and the Irish Working Class, 1830-1945* (Palgrave Macmillan, Basingstoke, 2005)

Kinealy, C., *Repeal and Revolution: 1848 in Ireland* (Manchester University Press, Manchester, 2009)

Legg, M-L., *Newspapers and Nationalism: The Irish Provincial Press, 1850-1892* (Four Courts Press, Dublin, 1999)

Legg, M.-L. (ed.), *Alfred Webb: The Autobiography of a Quaker Nationalist* (Cork University Press, Cork, 1999)

Lewis, S., *A History and Topography of Limerick City and County* (Mercier Press, Cork, 1980)

Lyons, F.S.L., *Ireland Since the Famine* (Weidenfeld & Nicolson, London, 1971)

Lysaght, P., 'Bartholomew Dowling', *Old Limerick Journal* (1996)

MacDonagh, O., *O'Connell: The Life of Daniel O'Connell 1775-1847* (Weidenfeld & Nicolson, London, 1991)

Mann, T., *Buddenbrooks* (Vintage, London, 1999)

Maume, P., 'Young Ireland, Arthur Griffith, and republican ideology: the question of continuity', *Éire-Ireland*, no. 34 (summer 1999)

Maye, B., *Arthur Griffith* (Griffith College Publications, Dublin, 1997)

McAllister, T.G., *Terence Bellew McManus: 1811(?)-1861* (St Patrick's College, Maynooth, 1972)

McGee, J.E., *The Men of '48* (Irish National Publishing House, Boston, 1881)

Miller, K.A., *Emigrants and Exiles* (Oxford University Press, Oxford, 1988)

Miller, K.A., *Ireland and Irish America: Culture, Class and Transatlantic Migration* (Field Day, Dublin, 2008)

Mitchel, J., *Jail Journal* (Burns, Oates & Washbourne, London, n.d.)

Mitchel, J., *Memoir of Thomas Devin Reilly* (P.M. Haverty, New York, 1857)

Mitchell, A., *Casement* (Haus Publishing, London, 2003)

Murphy, I., *Father Michael Meehan and the Ark of Kilbaha* (Cross, Ennis, 1980)

Namier, L., *1848: The Revolution of the Intellectuals* (Geoffrey Cumberlege, London, 1944)

Nolan, W., 'The Irish Confederation in County Tipperary in 1848', *Tipperary Historical Journal* (1998)

Nolan, W., 'The final days of Meagher's Irish uprising' in Hearne, J.M. and Cornish, R.T. (eds), *Thomas Francis Meagher: The Making of an Irish American* (Irish Academic Press, Dublin, 2006)

Ó Broin, L., *Charles Gavan Duffy: Patriot and Statesman* (James Duffy & Co., Dublin, 1967)

Ó Cathaoir, B., *John Blake Dillon: Young Irelander* (Irish Academic Press, Dublin, 1990)

Ó Cathaoir, B., *Young Irelander Abroad: The Diary of Charles Hart* (Cork University Press, Cork, 2003)

Ó Cathaoir, B., 'Dillon, John Blake (1814–1866)', *Oxford Dictionary of National Biography* (Oxford University Press, Oxford, 2004)

Ó Conchubhair, P., '"Not so much about the cabbage garden!": Kerry and the year of revolution – 1848', *The Kerry Magazine* (1998)

O'Donoghue, D.J., *Life and Writings of James Clarence Mangan* (M.H. Gill, Dublin, 1897)

O'Flaherty, L., *Famine* (Wolfhound Press, Dublin, 1994)

O'Flaherty, P., 'Michael Doheny: Young Irelander and Fenian', *The Irish Sword* (1987/1988)

Ó Grada, C., *Black '47 and Beyond: The Great Irish Famine in History, Economy and Memory* (Princeton University Press, Princeton, 1999)

O'Leary, J., *Recollections of Fenians and Fenianism*, 2 vols (Irish University Press, Shannon, 1969)

Ó Murchadha, C., 'Limerick Union workhouse during the Great Famine', *Old Limerick Journal* (1995)

O'Neill Daunt, W.J., *Personal Recollections of the Late Daniel O'Connell*, 2 vols (Chapman and Hall, London, 1848)

Osborne, C., *Verdi: A Life in the Theatre* (Weidenfeld & Nicolson, London, 1987)

Ó Tuathaigh, G., *Ireland Before the Famine* (Gill & Macmillan, Dublin, 1979)

Owens, G., 'Patrick O'Donohoe's narrative of the 1848 rising', *Tipperary Historical Journal* (1998)

Owens, G., 'Popular mobilisation and the rising of 1848: the clubs of the Irish Confederation' in Geary, L. (ed.), *Rebellion and Remembrance in Modern Ireland* (Four Courts Press, Dublin, 2001)

Palmer, S., *Police and Protest in England and Ireland: 1780–1850* (Cambridge University Press, Cambridge, 1988)

Pearl, C., *The Three Lives of Gavan Duffy* (New South Wales University Press, New South Wales, 1979)

Peter, A., *Dublin Fragments: Social and Historic* (Hodges, Figgis & Co., Dublin, 1925)

Phelan, J., *The Ardent Exile: The Life and Times of Thomas D'Arcy McGee* (Macmillan, Toronto, 1951)

Potter, M., *The Government and People of Ireland: The History of Limerick Corporation/City Council 1197–2006* (Limerick City Council, Limerick, 2006)

Quinn, J., *John Mitchel* (University College Dublin Press, Dublin, 2008)

Rapport, M., *1848: Year of Revolution* (Little, Brown, London, 2008)

Ryan, D., *The Fenian Chief: A Biography of James Stephens* (M.H. Gill & Son, Dublin, 1967)

Samson, J., *Chopin* (Oxford University Press, Oxford, 1998)

Savage, J., *'98 and '48: The Modern Revolutionary History and Literature of Ireland* (P.J. Kennedy, New York, 1882)

Sigmann, J., *1848: The Romantic and Democratic Revolutions in Europe* (George Allen & Unwin, London, 1973)

Sloan, R., *William Smith O'Brien and the Young Ireland Rebellion of 1848* (Four Courts Press, Dublin, 2000)

Sperber, J., *The European Revolutions, 1848–1851* (Cambridge University Press, Cambridge, 1995)

Storey, G. and Fielding, K.J. (eds), *The Letters of Charles Dickens: 1847–1849* (Clarendon Press, Oxford, 1981)

Thackeray, W.M., *A Collection of Letters of W.M. Thackeray, 1847–1855* (Smith, Elder & Co., London, 1887)

Thackeray, W.M., *The Irish Sketchbook of 1842* (Nonsuch, Dublin, 2005)

Vaughan, W.E. (ed.), *A New History of Ireland: Ireland Under the Union, 1801–70* (Clarendon Press, Oxford, 1989)

Walker, A., *Franz Liszt: The Weimar Years, 1848–1861* (Cornell University Press, New York, 1989)

Wilson, A.N., *The Victorians* (Arrow Books, London, 2003)

Young, G.M., *Victorian England: Portrait of an Age* (Oxford University Press, London, 1961)

INDEX